START-UP▲ GUITAR

It's never been easier to start playing guitar!

Published by
Wise Publications
14-15 Berners Street, London W1T 3LJ, UK.

Exclusive Distributors:
Music Sales Limited
Distribution Centre, Newmarket Road, Bury St Edmunds, Suffolk IP33 3YB, UK.
Music Sales Pty Limited
20 Resolution Drive, Caringbah, NSW 2229, Australia.

Order No. AM1002903
ISBN: 978-1-84938-981-5
This book © Copyright 2011 Wise Publications, a division of Music Sales Limited.

Adapted by David Harrison from an original book by Artie Traum.
Produced by shedwork.com
Design by Fresh Lemon.
Photography by Matthew Ward.
Models: Sagat Guirey and David Weston.
Edited by Tom Farncombe.
Printed in the EU.

With thanks to the City Lit, London.

Your Guarantee of Quality

www.musicsales.com

WISE PUBLICATIONS
part of The Music Sales Group

London / New York / Paris / Sydney / Copenhagen / Berlin / Madrid / Hong Kong / Tokyo

Playing a musical instrument is one of life's most rewarding pastimes and of all the instruments you could choose, the guitar might just be the most rewarding of all. Look at everything it has going for it: it's pretty easy to learn, it's portable, it's not too expensive, it sounds great, it comes in all shapes and sizes, and you can play virtually any kind of music on it, from classical to heavy metal!

If you're reading this and don't yet have a guitar, you're probably just about to get one.

The first question is 'which guitar?' Well, the truth is, as long as it works okay, any guitar will do when you're starting out, but it's a good idea to think about the style of music that you want to play, and choose a guitar accordingly.

You might want to take a trusted guitarist friend along to help you pick one out, but as long as you know your budget, have an idea of what sort you're after, and go to a reputable music store, you'll be fine.

CHOOSING A GUITAR

So what are the differences between the various kinds of guitar out there?

Steel String

The standard acoustic guitar sounds great without amplification—although many of them have a pickup built in, so you can put them through an amp for extra volume—and are traditionally played by folk-style guitarists. The steel strings give the guitar a 'twang' perfect for country and finger picking styles. However, they crop up all the time in rock and pop too.

It's a steel-string acoustic that you hear on early Bob Dylan records, 'Yesterday' by The Beatles and Oasis' 'Wonderwall'.

If you want a guitar you can take anywhere and play in lots of different styles, then this is the most obvious choice.

Tuning Peg
Headstock
Nut
Fret

Fingerboard
Fretboard

Fret Marker
Fret Wire

Neck

Body
Soundhole

Saddle
Bridge

The steel-string guitar is the perfect instrument for acoustic styles, whether you're strumming or finger picking.

Classical

The classical guitar (below) is a bit more specialised. Its mellow sound is used in flamenco, Latin styles such as bossa-nova and rumba and various other ethnic styles—but it also appears in all sorts of pop, from The Beatles ('And I Love Her') to Sting ('Shape Of My Heart'). Of course, it's used for classical music too. The main difference to the steel-string acoustic is that the classical guitar's nylon strings are much gentler on the fingertips. That advantage is more-or-less balanced by the wider fingerboard, which some players find a bit of a stretch.

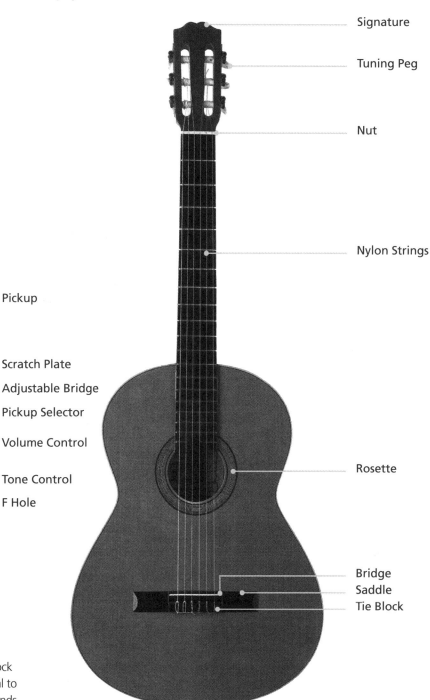

Signature
Tuning Peg
Nut
Nylon Strings
Rosette
Bridge
Saddle
Tie Block

Pickup
Scratch Plate
Adjustable Bridge
Pickup Selector
Volume Control
Tone Control
F Hole

Electric

The electric guitar (above) might instantly be associated with rock icons such as Jimi Hendrix, but amplified instruments are crucial to blues and jazz as well, and there is a vast range of possible sounds that you can achieve from the electric to suit many styles.
You will need an amp, and that's an added expense, but if you're serious about achieving a rock sound, then an electric guitar is probably for you. You'll add all sorts of effects pedals and other electronic gizmos to your arsenal as you begin to discover the world of amplified guitar, but a small practice amp is fine to start with.

If you're not familiar with the sound of the classical guitar, try listening to Rodrigo's 'Concierto De Aranjuez'.

GETTING STARTED

Once you've got a guitar, there are a few things to sort out: first of all, you'll need to find somewhere to practise.

In the next section we'll look at posture, but for now try to find a chair that's not too low—definitely not an armchair or couch—so you can just about place your feet on the floor. Some people like to use a bar stool with a foot rail.

Whatever chair you choose, you might well find that a strap helps to support the guitar, taking the strain off your arms.

A comfortable place to sit is a must, and a strap helps to take the weight off.

You'll also need a tuner: electronic tuners are cheap and easy to use, and very accurate. Some clip on to your guitar, and others can be put on a desk in front of you.

If you have an electric guitar, you'll probably need to plug the guitar into the tuner with a cable. We'll look at how to tune the guitar in a while.

There are a lot of other things you *could* buy at this point: picks and a capo for instance, but the only other thing you should really have is a spare set of strings.

They don't often break, but when they do, it's good to know that you have a replacement handy right away.

You should also have a music stand, and—to save your guitar from getting knocked over—a guitar stand.

Oh, and a nail file! Keep your left-hand finger-nails short and clean and don't allow your right-hand fingernails to get too long or to split.

A stool like this is perfect for sitting to play the guitar.

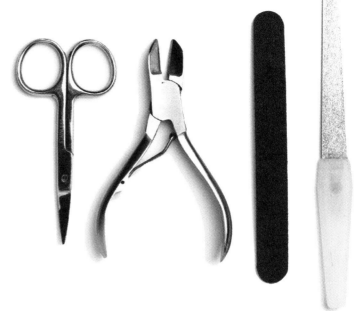

It's worth keeping a spare set of strings (above). Classical, electric and steel-string acoustic guitars require specific types of strings. Let your local music store recommend the right type for you.

Picks (below) are a good choice for strumming and picking to get a louder sound and to save your nails.

Carry a small selection of nailcare items in your case (above).

An electronic tuner is simple to use and very accurate (below).

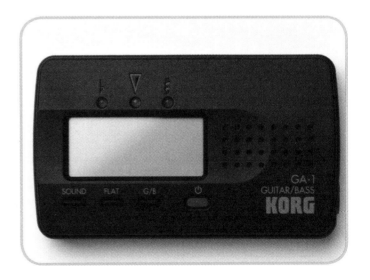

HOLDING THE GUITAR

Although the guitar is a folk instrument, and there are lots of opinions on the way it should be held, one thing is sure: it has to feel comfortable when you are playing.

You're bound to get a little tired, especially at the start, but having good technique will minimise any potential problems.

Sit with your feet flat on the floor, or upright on a stool, and perch a bit at the front of the seat.

The guitar should rest on your right thigh, and hopefully you'll find it more-or-less balances there with just a little help from your left hand, which lightly grips the neck.

The front of the guitar should face away from you so you can't see it if you look down.

Whether standing or sitting, the left-hand position is important. The thumb should stay behind the neck, positioned at about the 2nd fret, and the hand should form a gentle curve so that the fingers can come down onto the fretboard at right angles.

This way, you can be sure that the fingertips are making contact with just the strings they need to touch, and not getting in the way of any of the others.

TOP TIP ✓

A well-made guitar is balanced so that it should stay on your lap with the minimum of effort.

This means that your arms and hands will be free to concentrate on playing rather than holding the guitar tight.

Spend time experimenting with your guitar until you're able to keep it in position without thinking about it.

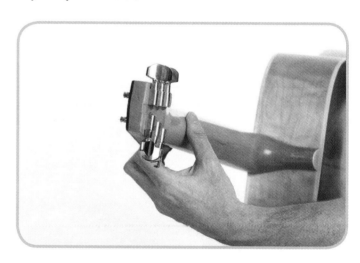

The right hand, whether strumming or picking, should hang loosely over the front of the guitar at the sound hole (if your guitar is acoustic) or the pickups (if it's an electric).

Make sure your body is relaxed, so you don't develop strains. If you feel any part of you getting sore, take a little rest and have a look to see whether you can change anything about the way you're holding the guitar that will help.

As you start to learn new chords, strumming techniques or anything else involving your hands, there will be a great temptation to look down at your hands to make sure they're in the right place.

But, since you shouldn't be able to see the front of the guitar if you're holding it right, you'd need to hunch right over or twist the guitar up towards you before you can see what you're doing. So get used to feeling for the right position with your fingers.

Try sitting with a mirror in front of you—even a make-up mirror placed on a desk or music stand should help. This way you can check your hand position without compromising your posture and technique.

With a music stand, any music books, song sheets or other paper can be held at eye level, and you should be able to keep a comfortable position for longer periods than if you had to keep looking down at your work.

TUNING

Getting the guitar in tune is a crucial skill. There are various methods, but they all involve adjusting the pitch of the open (unfretted) strings by turning the tuning pegs to tighten or loosen each string until it sounds the correct note. Let's look at the main methods.

Tuning the thicker strings can pull on the guitar neck enough to affect all the other strings, so there's no point in carefully tuning the thinner strings only to have to retune them once you've tuned the thicker ones.

Let's look at the sound source method first. These diagrams show the notes you need on the piano, the equivalent musical notation, and the appropriate strings on the guitar.

Notice how the strings are named (above right): the bottom string is the one that sounds lowest. The top string is the highest-sounding.

You can choose a sound source to tune against, such as a piano, pitch pipes, special audio tracks or a tuning fork; or else you can use an electronic tuner. which will tell you when your guitar is in tune.

Either way, you should start with the thickest (also known as the *bottom*, or *sixth*) string, and work your way through the strings to the thinnest (*top*, or *first*).

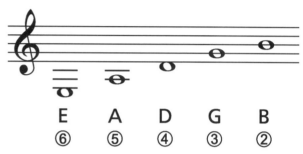

By the way: in guitar notation, notes are written an octave higher than the actual sounding pitch.

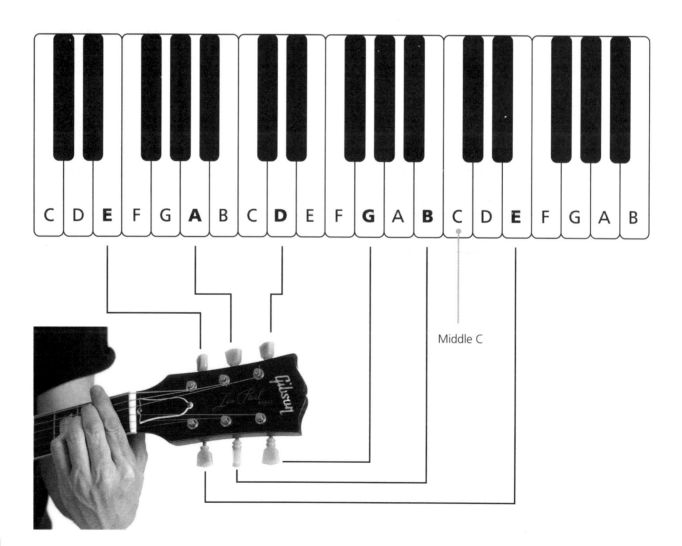

Middle C

Relative Tuning

If you tune the bottom string accurately, you can then use that string to tune the others.

Here's how it works:

- Place a finger on the 5th fret of the bottom (sixth) string—this will give you the note you need (A) to tune the open fifth string.

- Once that's done, play a note on the 5th fret of the fifth string. It'll be D, which is the note you need for the open fourth string.

- And again, play a note on the 5th fret of the fourth string to give you the note you need (G) for the open third string.

- Now the sequence changes: this time, play a note on the 4th fret of the third string to sound B, which is the correct note for the open second string.

- Finally, play a note on the 5th fret of the second string to sound E, which is the note you'll need to tune the top string.

Although it might seem a bit fiddly, this method is great for checking a single string if you're in the middle of playing, and since it relies on your ears it's great training too... check the diagram below for fret positions for each of the reference notes.

Clip-on style tuners are especially convenient (see the section on electronic tuners, below).

Electronic Tuners

Using an electronic tuner has lots of advantages: they're pretty fool-proof, and very precise.

And, if you're tuning in a noisy situation, plugging a tuner in or attaching it to the guitar means you can tune even if you can't hear the guitar properly.

Play the bottom string, and the device will show you on its display whether you're low or high.

Tune the string in the right direction and, when it's up to pitch, the display will let you know. Simply move on to the next string and so on, until the instrument is tuned.

PRACTICE

It's a good idea to get into a realistic practice routine right away. Practice is the key to improving on the guitar, but it can also be the source of much frustration.

Here are a few tips to help you practise more effectively:

- A little practice every day is much more valuable than a finger-numbing mammoth session once a week.

- Keep a check on your posture and technique, to avoid any niggles creeping into your playing.

- Start slowly and build up: there will be a little wear and tear on your fingers to begin with, and it will take a bit of time to build up the calluses on your left finger tips—it's easy to overdo it, especially at the beginning.

- Set a target for each practice session, and make it realistic. Some people keep a practice diary, making a note of things to try in the next session. It's a great way to record your progress.

- Set aside time to play for fun. Keep it separate from your practice time, but make sure you sit and strum once in a while for no particular reason: after all, it's why you're learning to play guitar!

Practising a little each day is the best way to build up your technique and confidence steadily.

READING CHORD DIAGRAMS

The first thing you'll learn to play on the guitar are chords, which are groups of notes strummed together. Chords are written down using chord diagrams, or chord *boxes*.

Here's how they look:

The thicker line at the top is the nut—the white bone or hard plastic piece at the top of the guitar neck.

The horizontal lines are frets—the wire divisions along the fingerboard.

The vertical lines are the strings, and the dark dots show where fingers are placed on the strings.

If an X appears above a string, this string shouldn't be played, and with an O, the string is played 'open': without any fingers on it.

Compare the top of the neck with the chord box

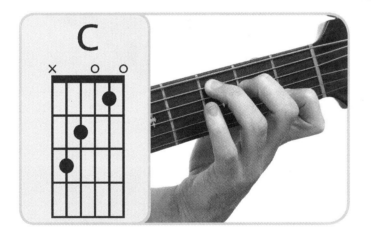

Here's how the chord boxes are used in this book—they are displayed upright, accompanied by a photograph of the fingers in a natural, horizontal position. Compare the diagram with the photograph to see how they relate.

Left-hander?

If you happen to be left-handed, there's nothing standing in your way to playing the guitar. There are plenty of left-handed guitars out there, and as you work through this book, you'll simply need to reverse everything you see.

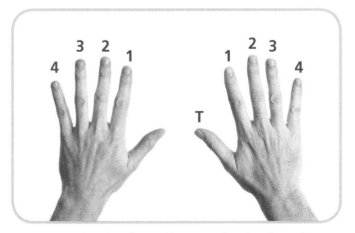

Guitarists number their fingers like so. T is for 'thumb', and although both hands are labelled the same way, the 4th finger of the right hand is hardly ever used.

Now you're ready to get playing. So let's have a look at your first chords.

YOUR FIRST TWO CHORDS

To start playing songs, you only need to know two chords, so let's make a start with A and E. Remember, the diagrams are shown upright, with the thick line at the top representing the nut—the piece at the top of the neck.

Try placing the 1st finger on the 2nd fret of the fourth string, like this:

Now, add the 2nd and 3rd fingers on the third and second strings, also on the 2nd fret, like so:

You're now fingering an A chord. If you brush down lightly across the strings with your right thumb, you'll hear the result. You may find that some of the notes are a bit muffled, so see if you can adjust the fingers until each note sounds out clearly.

You might need to ensure your thumb is in just the right place at the back of the neck to give your fingers the best possible chance of coming down onto the fingerboard at an angle approaching perpendicular: otherwise you risk touching more than one string with each finger.

We'll begin by taking a close look at the way a single finger should sit on the fretboard. The fingertip should come down at right angles to the fretboard onto the string just behind the fretwire. If you find you're struggling to make a note sound without a huge effort, go back and check this basic finger position (see below).

Press the strings down as near as you can to the fret without them actually being on the fret. If you're pressing very hard to get a clear sound, there might be something a bit wrong with your finger position, so stop again and check that.

Try to bring the fingertip down onto the string just behind the fretwire.

For now your right hand can simply curl up slightly and strum down across the strings. We'll get into some more advanced strumming soon, but for now just brush down with the thumb.

Brushing the strings with the thumb is a good way to hear how chords sound.

Give the A chord another go, and this time try to strum down without touching the bottom string. Ideally A doesn't use the bottom string, as you can see in the diagram.

Once you're happy with it (and it doesn't have to be perfect for now) we'll move on to our second chord, the chord of E.

E is a great chord for bringing out the full character of your guitar. It uses all six strings, and it looks like this:

Although it might not seem very helpful at the moment, make a note of the position of the 2nd and 3rd fingers relative to each other. They're next door to one another, just as they were for the A chord.

The fact is, playing chords on the guitar is easy enough: the challenge is often changing from one chord to another. Finding any similarities you can between chord shapes will give you a head start, and that's just what we're going to do now.

TOP TIP ✓

Changing from one chord shape to another is often more of a challenge than playing chord shapes on their own. Try to find any useful similarities between shapes to make the job easier.

CHORD CHANGES AND YOUR FIRST SONG

Take a look at this piece of music: it's four 'bars' long, and alternates between the chord of A and the chord of E.

Play the exercise slowly through, and try to keep a steady beat.

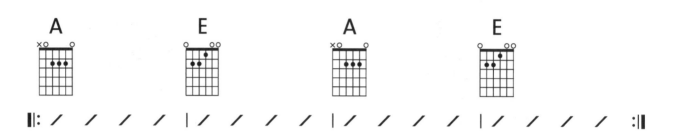

Strum down each time you see a slash (/). Each slash represents a single beat of music.

Four strums of A will make a *bar*, and then it's time to play a bar of E.

The first few times, you might prefer to strum once on A, and count the four beats out while you change to E. Try to play the E chord right at the beginning of the new bar.

Count again and change back to A, and so on. Once you have done it several times, you'll be able to strum slowly through, once on each beat without having to pause to change the shapes.

Notice the double bar lines with dots:

These are repeat marks, and are found either side of a repeated section of music. In this case, they indicate simply that the whole of the music should be played again.

Check the chord diagram for A once more, and remember not to play the bottom string when you strum. If you happen to strum the bottom string too, it's not going to sound too terrible on an A chord, but there are times where it will sound messy and clash with the music.

Get into the habit of learning just which strings are needed for each new chord you see, and spend a little while seeing just how your strumming hand moves across the strings.

Eventually you'll be able to miss out the bottom string without even thinking.

When you're reasonably happy with the way things are going, you'll be ready to tackle your first song (opposite).

It uses both the chords you've just been playing, A and E.

There are rhythm slashes as before, and this time arrows are added to show you to strum down on each beat.

You don't need to read music notation to play the song on the next page: just follow the strums for the chords and sing the words.

If any of the songs in this book aren't familiar to you, listen to some recordings to learn the tune.

Try playing this gospel standard using the two chords. To start with, you might try just playing each chord once, clearly, when it appears, and count through until it's time to play the next new chord. As you play, let your ears help you to tell which chord to play.

Soon you'll start to predict when the new chord comes by the sound it should make.

Take the song slowly, and try to move smoothly between chords. Check that your fingers are making the most efficient and accurate movements possible.

As for the right hand, again the movement should be smooth and steady. It's enough just to stroke the strings gently with the thumb.

Down by the Riverside

Gon-na lay down my bur - den,_ down by the ri-ver- side,_

down by the ri-ver- side,_ down by the ri-ver- side._ Gon-na

lay down my bur - den,_ down by the ri-ver - side,_ and

stu - dy war no more._

STARTING TO PICK

Now that you've conquered your first song, let's look at a more interesting way to strum. In fact, you're going to strum and pick. Picking is an essential part of guitar technique, especially in **acoustic styles such as country and folk, and it's widely used in blues, ragtime and some types of jazz too, so it's worth spending some time on it.**

In this next exercise, the thumb is going to pick just the bottom string of the chord on the first beat, and again on the third beat. The lowest note of a chord is called the bass note. Now, the bass note of the A chord is on the fifth string, but on the E chord it's the sixth string.

Alternate the picked bass notes with strummed chords by brushing the strings down with the backs of the fingernails. Hold the hand loosely, and allow the nails to pass smoothly across the strings. The hand motion should come from the wrist, which should be relaxed.

On beats 2 and 4, strum the whole chord as before. Try this exercise, slowly and steadily at first:

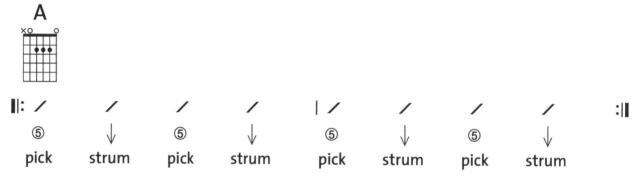

A

‖: /   /   /   / | /   /   /   /   :‖

⑤   ↓   ⑤   ↓   ⑤   ↓   ⑤   ↓

pick   strum   pick   strum   pick   strum   pick   strum

Try to keep the rhythm steady and smooth.
Take it slowly at first, gradually increasing the tempo.

Now try the same thing on the E chord:

E

‖: /   /   /   / | /   /   /   /   :‖

⑥   ↓   ⑥   ↓   ⑥   ↓   ⑥   ↓

Once you are happy with the basic strum, you could try alternating between two bass notes on two different strings. Have a look at the next exercise (below).

This time, pick and strum the A chord as before, but alternate with the thumb between the fifth string and the sixth string. It'll create a rhythmic bass line in a country style reminiscent of the music of Johnny Cash.

Try not to let each thumbed note ring out for more than one beat to keep the pattern sounding clean.

A

```
‖: /      /      /      /   | /      /      /      /   :‖
   ⑤      ↓      ⑥      ↓      ⑤      ↓      ⑥      ↓
```

Then try alternating the bass on the E chord. This time, pick the sixth string on the first beat, and change to the fifth string on the third beat. You'll achieve a similar sound to the previous exercise:

E

```
‖: /      /      /      /   | /      /      /      /   :‖
   ⑥      ↓      ⑤      ↓      ⑥      ↓      ⑤      ↓
```

Finally, let's try another chord shape.

This one goes well with A and E. It's the chord of D. It only uses four strings, so take care when strumming not to play the bottom two strings by mistake. Here it is:

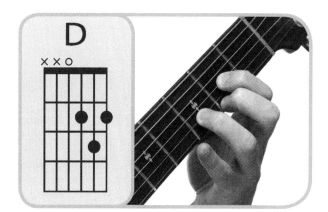

If you like, you could try playing the alternating bass you just looked at. For D, you would alternate between the fourth and fifth strings:

D

```
‖: /      /      /      /   | /      /      /      /   :‖
   ④      ↓      ⑤      ↓      ④      ↓      ⑤      ↓
```

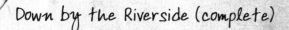
Down by the Riverside (complete)

Now that you know A, E and D, you can tackle the rest of 'Down by the Riverside'.

This time it's marked with the alternating bass strumming, too.

Gon-na lay down my bur - den,_ down by the ri-ver - side,_

down by the ri-ver - side,_ down by the ri-ver - side. Gon-na

lay down my bur - den,_ down by the ri-ver - side,_ and

stu - dy war no more._____ Ain't gon - na

Finish the song with three strums.

Here are three more songs that just use
the chords of A, D and E. They'll give you
a chance to practise changing between the
chords and to pick & strum steadily.

Will the Circle Be Unbroken

Will the cir - cle   be un - brok - en,   by and

by, Lord, by and   by?_____   There's a   bet - ter   home a -

- wait - ing   in the sky, Lord,   in the   sky.

Finish this song with one strum, and let it
ring for three beats.

The Banks of the Ohio

'The Streets of Laredo' (opposite) has three beats to the bar, which creates quite a different feel.

Because there aren't an even number of beats, the *pick-strum, pick-strum* pattern won't work. So let's look at an alternative.

The simplest solution is to pick the bass note of the chord on the first beat as before, and strum the other two beats. This kind of rhythm is often referred to as 'boom ching ching' in folk and country circles:

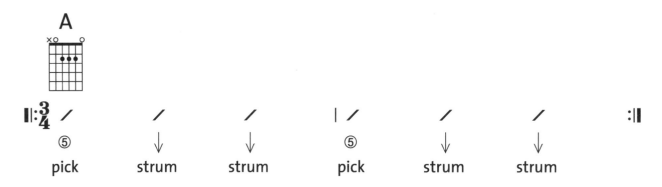

This will work fine for all three of our chords. Just remember to adjust the bass note picking for each chord: fifth string for A, fourth for D and sixth for E.

In cases where a chord lasts for more than one bar, you can alternate the bass note on the first beat of the subsequent bar:

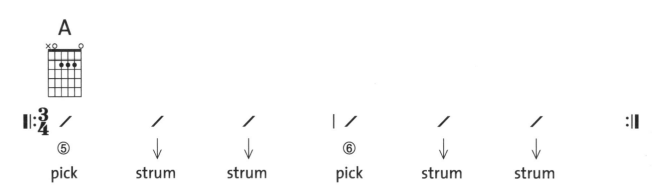

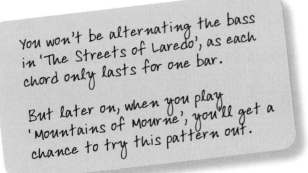

You won't be alternating the bass in 'The Streets of Laredo', as each chord only lasts for one bar.

But later on, when you play 'Mountains of Mourne', you'll get a chance to try this pattern out.

The Streets of Laredo

TO PICK OR NOT TO PICK

Various guitar styles have traditionally been associated with different types of picks. Let's look at the main types.

The single, flat pick, usually called a *flatpick*, or *plectrum*, is widely used among both electric and acoustic guitarists. Many people like the crisp, bright sound they can achieve.

For harder rock lead lines with very light strings, a stiffer, thicker pick might be more suitable, while for strumming lightly on the relatively thick strings of a steel-string acoustic, a light, flexible pick is a better bet.

Jazz guitarists seem to like the small, hard plectrums that allow them to target strumming and lead lines.

Finger picking guitarists who need to pick several strings at once, on the other hand, often go for sets of metal or plastic picks that fit around the fingers and thumb.

Some people prefer to use their nails to pick and strum. If you plan to do this, it pays to carry a nail file and scissors with you to keep your nails in shape.

However, if you'd prefer to use a pick, there's a baffling array of different types available. None are expensive, so the best approach is probably just to buy a variety and try them out.

Below is a selection of different types.

A standard nylon pick is the type used by most people. A medium gauge of 0.6 mm is about average. Many guitarists will use a thicker pick on lighter strings, and a thinner pick on heavier strings.

A small, thick pick is the type favoured by many jazz guitarists.

Metal and plastic picks that fit directly onto the fingers are a specialist type used by finger picking guitarists in folk, blues and country styles.

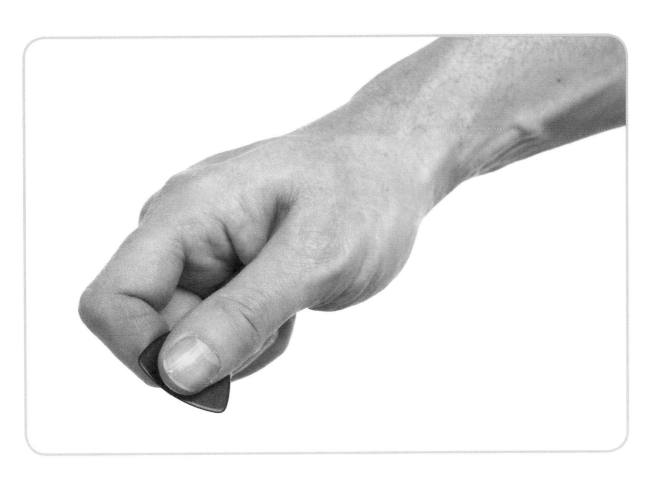

Now, get back to 'Will the Circle Be Unbroken' (page 22) and play it using a plectrum. Hold the pick between your right thumb and index finger—not too tight, but not too loose either. You want to exert a fair amount of pressure without overdoing it.

As you can see, only a small part of the pick should project beyond the edges of your thumb and finger. Your wrist should stay relaxed. To get the feeling, shake the pick as if you were shaking a thermometer.

Now, hit the fifth string while holding an A chord and strum down as you did before. Is the sound clean? Can you hear all of the notes? If the sound is muddy, don't despair. You will get the hang of the pick eventually, if you keep at it.

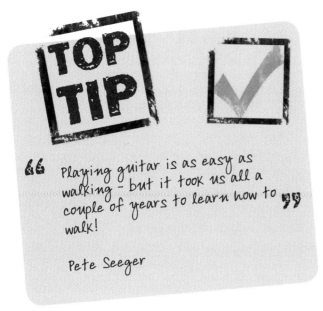

TOP TIP ✓

"Playing guitar is as easy as walking – but it took us all a couple of years to learn how to walk!

Pete Seeger

RED RIVER VALLEY

Here's another new chord. It's a variation on the E shape we've already looked at, called E7. You can play it by taking a finger away from the E shape:

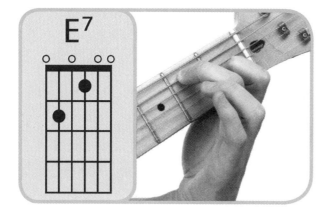

You could also try an optional extra note on the 2nd string:

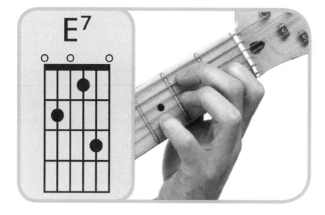

For this song, we haven't included notation for the picking and strumming pattern.

Strum as before, with the optional alternating bass picking—but get used to playing the correct bass strings from memory: it'll stick in your mind much quicker that way.

Give it a go with this new song: it uses all the chords you've tried so far, and goes at a fairly brisk pace.

Try using all the alternating bass picking if you like, but you might need to play it through slowly a few times first to make a note of which bass notes to use.

The bass notes for E7 are the same as those for E.

In the second line, notice the change from E to E7: play the E shape, and then lift off the 2nd finger as you move to E7. You can alternate the bass in the same way for both chords, which will create continuity.

2.
Won't you think of this valley you're leaving,
Oh, how lonely, how sad it will be.
Oh, think of the fond heart you're breaking,
And the grief you are causing to me.

3.
From this valley they say you are going,
When you go, may your darling go to?
Would you leave her behind unprotected,
When she loves no other but you?

4.
I have promised you, darling, that never
Will a word from my lips cause you,
And my life, it will be yours for ever,
If you only will love me again.

Red River Valley

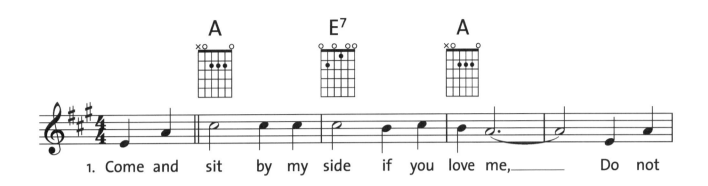

1. Come and sit by my side if you love me,_____ Do not

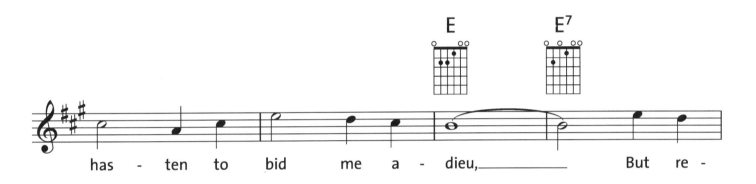

has - ten to bid me a - dieu,_____ But re -

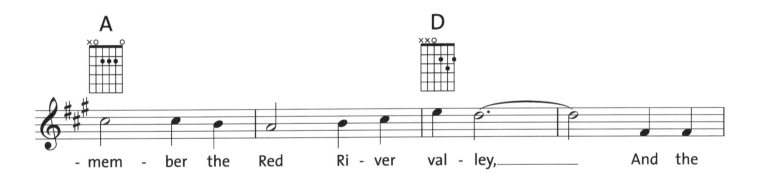

- mem - ber the Red Ri - ver val - ley,_____ And the

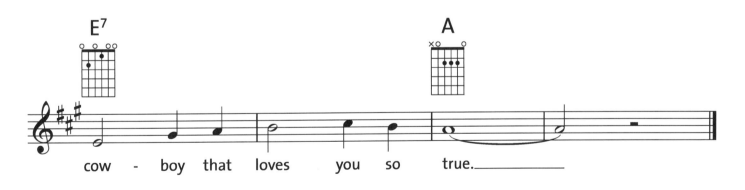

cow - boy that loves you so true._____

SHE'LL BE COMING 'ROUND THE MOUNTAIN

All the music we've played so far is in the key of A: hopefully you can hear how it comes to rest on the final A chord of the song each time. A, D and E, plus E7, are all you'll need to play countless songs in this key.

To play in other keys, you simply need to find similar groups of chords. Try these chords, to play in the key of D.

The new shape of G needs special care. You might find it easist to put the little finger into position first, then move the 2nd and 3rd fingers into place.

Practise moving from G to D and back again several times, and check that your thumb is sitting at the back of the neck to give your fingers the support they need.

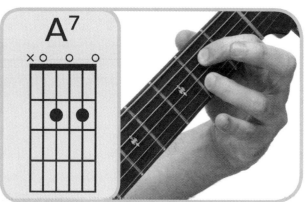

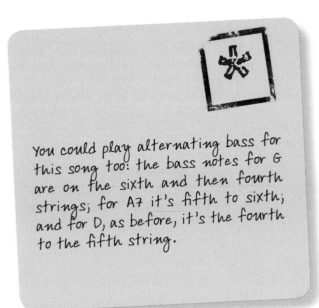

You could play alternating bass for this song too: the bass notes for G are on the sixth and then fourth strings; for A7 it's fifth to sixth; and for D, as before, it's the fourth to the fifth string.

2.
She'll be driving six white horses when she comes,
She'll be driving six white horses when she comes,
She'll be driving six white horses, driving six white horses,
She'll be driving six white horses when she comes.

3.
Oh, we'll all go out to meet her when she comes,
Oh, we'll all go out to meet her when she comes,
Oh, we'll all go out to meet her, all go out to meet her,
Oh, we'll all go out to meet her when she comes.

4.
She'll be wearing a blue bonnet when she comes,
She'll be wearing a blue bonnet when she comes,
She'll be wearing a blue bonnet, wearing a blue bonnet,
She'll be wearing a blue bonnet when she comes.

She'll be Coming 'Round the Mountain

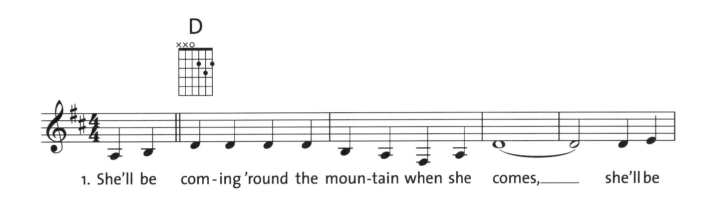

1. She'll be com-ing 'round the moun-tain when she comes,_____ she'll be

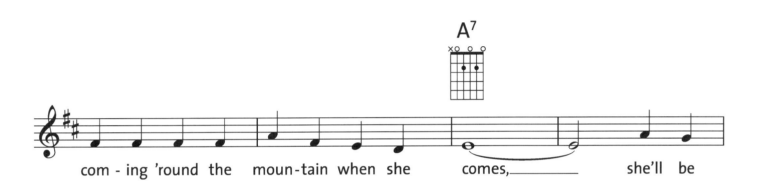

com-ing 'round the moun-tain when she comes,_____ she'll be

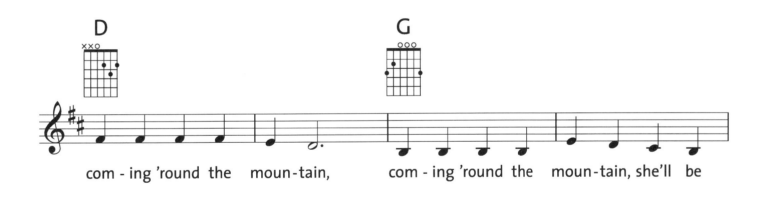

com-ing 'round the moun-tain, com-ing 'round the moun-tain, she'll be

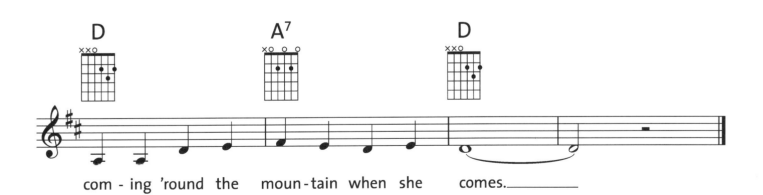

com-ing 'round the moun-tain when she comes._____

PLAYING IN MORE KEYS

Now here are some chords for the key of C.

For F, place the 1st finger across the 1st fret of both the first and second strings. This is known as a *barre*.

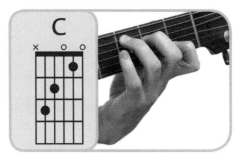

These chords, two of which we've already played, will give you a group for G:

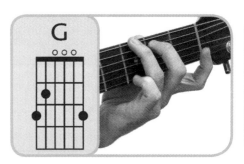

As you already know E and A, you only need one more chord to play in the key of E:

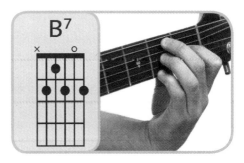

Alternate the bass for B7 as follows:

Play the standard bass note on the first beat. Then move the 2nd finger over to the 2nd fret of the bottom string, and play the new bass note on beat 3.

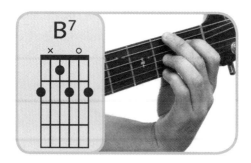

E

In the next song, strum down on the **second and fourth beats as before, but this time follow it with an up-strum half a beat later, as shown. It'll create more rhythmic interest and help the song flow better.**

If you're using a pick, hold it loosely **and strum gently. If you're strumming with your fingers, the up-strums should be played with the back of the thumbnail, and the down-strums with the backs of the fingernails.**

⑥   ↓   ↑   ⑤   ↓   ↑   ⑥   ↓   ↓   ⑤   ↓   ↑

Mama Don't Allow

Ma-ma don't al-low no   gui-tar play-in' round here.

Ma-ma don't al-low no   gui-tar play-in' round here.

I don't care what   Ma-ma don't al-low, gon-na pick my gui-tar,   a - ny-how.

Ma-ma don't al-low no   gui-tar_ play-in' round here.

MINOR CHORDS

Now it's time to try a new type of chord, the minor chord. Minor chords have a different sound, but are often used in combination with the ones we've already covered.

Minor chords are indicated by the letter 'm' after the chord name as shown below.

  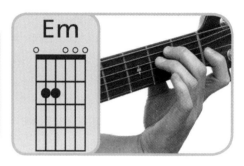

Try this chord sequence to hear how major and minor chords can be combined. This first example is in the key of C:

This sequence is used a lot in pop and rock, and was especially popular in rock 'n' roll ballads.

Now try it in G:

Minor chords also crop up in sad blues songs like this next one. Strum each beat rhythmically and slowly, without alternating the bass picking.

St. James Infirmary Blues

MORE ALTERNATING BASS

The next song uses just two chords. For D minor, alternate the bass from the fouth string to the fifth.

For C, you'll need to move the 3rd finger down to the 3rd fret of the sixth string for the third beat, a little like the way the bass note changed for B7 in 'Mama Don't Allow' on page 33. This is shown in the two pictures on the right.

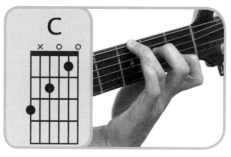

Play an alternating bass for the chord of C between the fifth and sixth strings on the 3rd fret.

Try alternating between the bass notes for each chord you know, and see if you can memorise which pairs of strings are required for each chord shape. Eventually, you'll see a pattern emerging:

4- or 5-string chords

On any chord where the bass note is on the fourth or fifth strings, alternate between the bass note and the note on the next string down, on the same fret (or open string).

Take a look at the chords of C, Am and D, for example, and check this pattern. It'll work for any major or minor chord, and should be very useful.

6-string chords

If you're playing a 6-string chord, it's likely either to be an E-type or a G-type.

- For G chords (G, G7 etc.) alternate from the sixth to the fourth strings.

- For E chords (E, Em, E7 etc.) alternate from the sixth to the fifth strings.

Drunken Sailor

READING TABLATURE

For strumming chords, diagrams showing left-hand finger positions are sufficient. But when it comes to finger picking, guitarists use a more complete notation system. This is tablature, or *tab*.

Tablature is a musical notation system for stringed instruments that shows the performer exactly where to play each note on the fretboard. This notation is used instead of standard notation, which shows the actual pitches.

If you haven't yet learned to read either system, you should try learning tablature first. It's easier to learn, and it's mandatory for much guitar music, especially for alternate tunings.

The tablature system consists of six horizontal lines, each representing a guitar string. The bass string is the bottom line of the tablature staff, and the treble string is the top line.

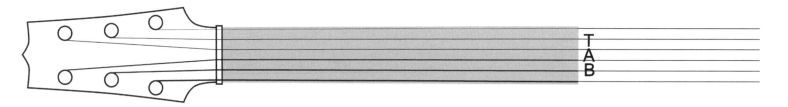

This layout is inverted from the actual string positions on the instrument. Here, the high-pitched notes lie high on the staff and the low-pitched notes lie low on the staff. In this way tablature resembles standard notation.

A number on a line indicates at which fret to depress that string. This example (right) describes all six strings of an E7 shape, picked in turn, starting with the lowest.

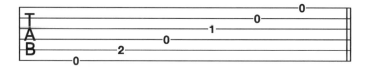

Sometimes, the stems and beams above or below the staff denote the rhythm. In this example, the rhythm is a series of eighth notes.

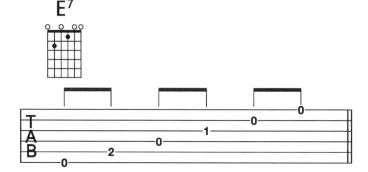

Where two or more notes are played simultaneously, they are
stacked up on the stave.

Compare these diagrams with the equivalent notes shown in tab
to see how this works.

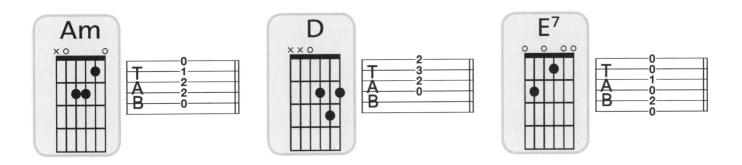

The next example shows notes of various chords played one after
the other. This type of pattern is known as an *arpeggio*. Compare
the chord diagrams with the notation, and pick the passage slowly
through until the arpeggios are smooth.

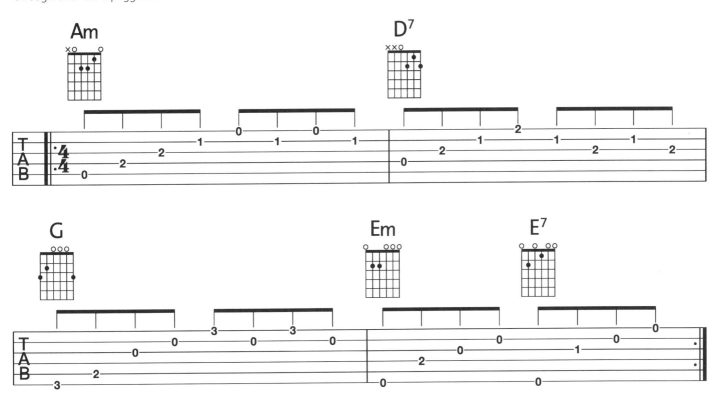

Remember: it can be more of a challenge
to play smoothly at a slower tempo,
because there's no chance of bluffing
your way through!

FINGER PICKING

To start with, you strummed all the notes of the chord at once. Then, we added picked bass notes. Now we'll play the notes of the chord individually to create finger picking patterns. Finger picking is perhaps the most satisfying of all guitar styles, and it is one of the most challenging to master.

Your thumb is the pivot point of all finger picking. Let's build up a pattern little by little on an E chord. Eventually the pattern will require your right thumb, together with the 1st, 2nd and 3rd fingers.

As you try these exercises, be sure to use the correct finger each time.

Start by slowly moving your thumb back and forth from the sixth string to the fifth string.

Give two beats to each bass note:

There are endless ways to approach this technique: from the thumping blues of Robert Johnson, Skip James, and Ry Cooder; the subtle melodic ideas of Doc Watson and Chet Atkins; to the energetic, percussive pyrotechnics of Newton Faulkner and Tommy Emmanuel.

The fingers will remain on the top three strings throughout, with the thumb moving to whichever string is needed for the correct bass note.

E

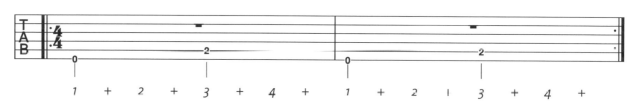

Now, add a note on the second string played at the same time as the bass notes—every two beats. Use your 2nd finger for these second-string notes:

E

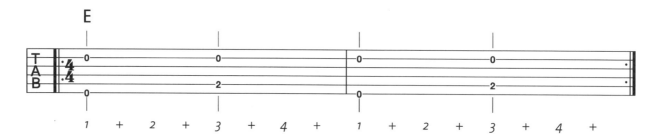

Next, add notes in between on the top string, with the 3rd finger. Play this through until it 'sits' in your fingers (ex. 3).

Count 'I and 2 and 3 and 4 and' as you start to play these exercises to keep the rhythm steady.

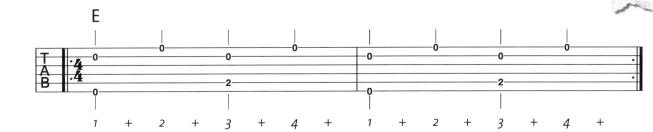

Try adding a note on the third string, played with the 1st finger, together with the 3rd-finger notes.

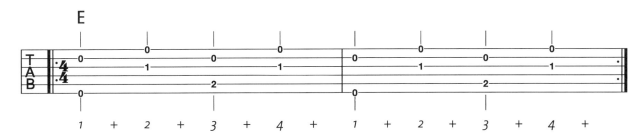

When that's smooth, move on to the next example. Here, the same notes are played, but the finger pattern is broken up over the thumb bass notes. This makes a great ragtime-style picking pattern:

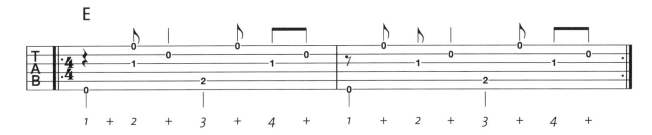

Experiment with different accents, and at different speeds. You'll be surprised how something as simple as changing the way the notes are accented can change the feel of the pattern. Finally, here's the same pattern on A and B7:

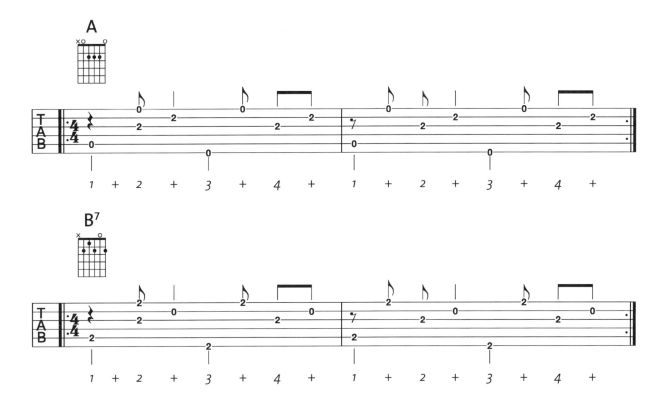

Once you're comfortable with this pattern, try it on songs throughout the book. Keep the fingers on the top three strings, and be sure to vary the bass notes (picked with the thumb) according to the different chords.

Feel free to experiment with strumming and picking patterns. You could even write down patterns that you particularly like.

PICKING IN 3/4

Like 'Streets of Laredo', this next song has three beats to the bar. Most chords last at least two bars each, so it's ideal for an alternating bass pattern like the one below.

If you're not sure how to alternate some of the bass notes, take another look at bottom of page 36, which gives you the 'rules' for alternating bass.

The song splits into two sections: try picking the first part, and strumming the second part for contrast.

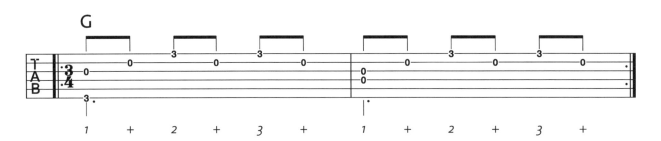

Mountains of Mourne

1. Oh Mar - y, this Lon - don's a won - der - ful sight, with
2. I be - lieve that when writ - ing a wish you ex - pressed as to
3. There's beau - ti - ful girls here, oh nev - er you mind, with

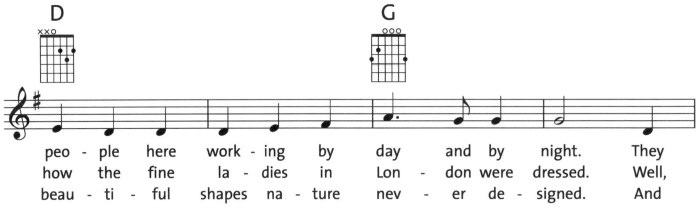

peo - ple here work - ing by day and by night. They
how the fine la - dies in Lon - don were dressed. Well,
beau - ti - ful shapes na - ture nev - er de - signed. And

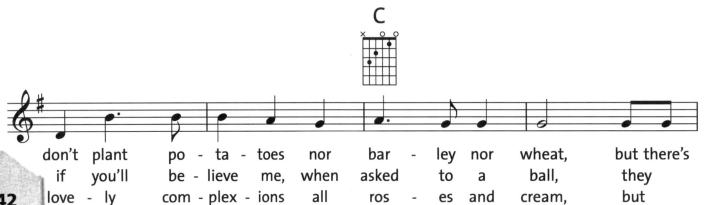

don't plant po - ta - toes nor bar - ley nor wheat, but there's
if you'll be - lieve me, when asked to a ball, they
love - ly com - plex - ions all ros - es and cream, but

MORE SONGS

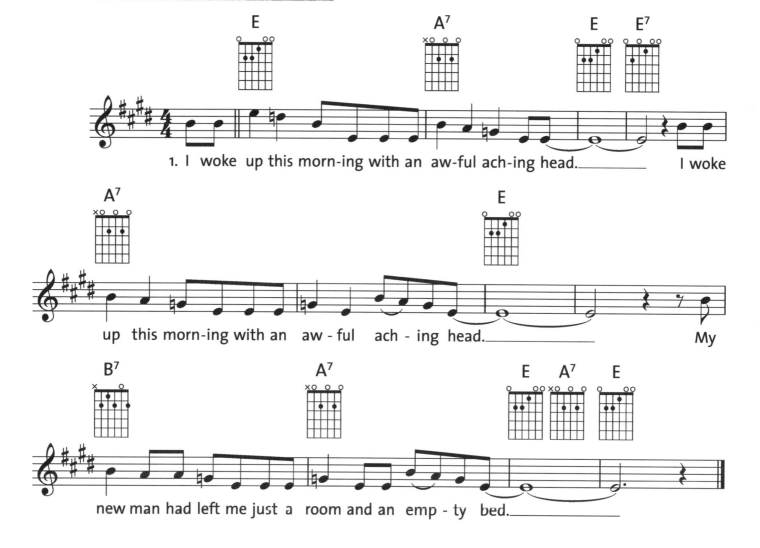

1. I woke up this morn-ing with an aw-ful ach-ing head._____ I woke
up this morn-ing with an aw - ful ach - ing head._____ My
new man had left me just a room and an emp - ty bed._____

2.
He's a coffee grinder—grinding all the time
He's a coffee grinder—grinding all the time
He can grind my coffee, 'cause he's got a brand-new grind.
3.
If you get good loving, never go and spread the news
If you get good loving, never go and spread the news
Gals will double-cross you and leave you with the empty bed blues.

Using the picking pattern on page 41, try accenting some of the off-beat notes to create a syncopated feel, in the style of a ragtime beat: and, like a rag, it shouldn't be played too fast...

Freight Train

1. Freight train, freight train run so fast,____

Freight train, freight train run so fast.____

Please don't tell what__ train I'm on,____ They won't

know what__ route I've gone._____

2.
When I'm dead and in my grave,
No more good times will I crave.
Place the stones at my head and feet,
And tell them all that I've gone to sleep.

3.
When I die, Lord, bury me deep,
Way down on old Chestnut Street,
So I can hear old Number Nine
As she comes rolling by.

The change from G – B7 – C might take some practice, but stick with it, as it's a great sound!

CHORD LIBRARY

 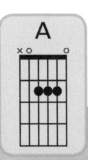 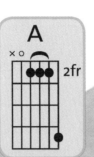 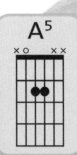 

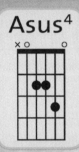 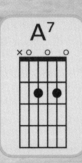 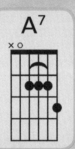  

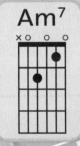 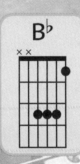 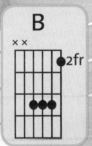 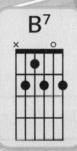 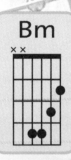

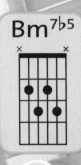 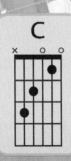 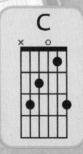  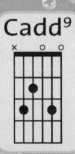

C⁷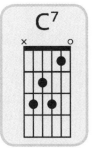

C⁹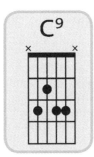

Caug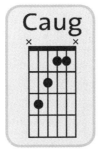

Cdim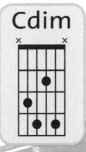

Cm

C#⁷

C#m

D

Dsus²

Dsus⁴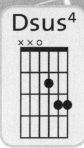

D⁷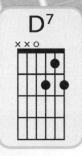

D⁷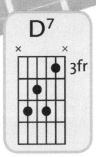

D⁹

Dm

Dm⁷

D#dim

E

Esus⁴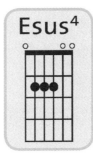

E⁵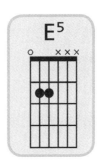

E⁷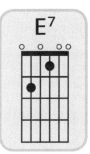

E⁷

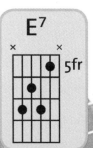
E⁷ 5fr

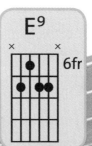
E⁹ 6fr

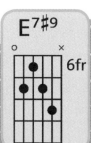
E⁷♯⁹ 6fr

Em

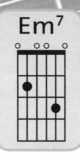
Em⁷

F

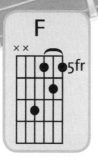
F 5fr

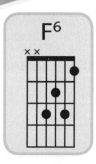
F⁶

Fmaj⁷

Faug

Fm

G

G

G⁶

G⁷

Gmaj⁷

Gmaj⁷ 2fr

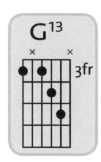
G¹³ 3fr

Gm 3fr

Jigsaw 3

ACKNOWLEDGEMENTS:

Jigsaw 3 was originally written for overseas work, based on themes and session titles by Janet
   Richards. Material selected for this book was contributed by Peter Ali, Peter Cooper, Brenda
   Cuthbert, Dinah Davis, Peter Empson, Dave Glover, Sue Harman, Priscilla Hodson, Stuart Holt,
   David Hooper, Jill Luce, Lysa Ludkin, Phil Moore, Trevor Ranger, Gill Reitsma, Fiona Revie, Pam Weaver
   and Elaine Williams;
Priscilla Hodson and Elaine Williams then revised, adapted and added to the material;
Matthew Slater did the typesetting, artwork and design;
and it was checked by Phil Moore, Rob Rawson and Tracey Welch!

Printed and bound in the United Kingdom by Stanley L Hunt (Printers) Ltd, Rushden, Northants.

Scriptures quoted from the New Century Version (Anglicised Edition) copyright © 1993 by
   Nelson Word Ltd, 9 Holdom Avenue, Bletchley, Milton Keynes, MK1 1QR, UK. (One verse quoted
   from the Good News Bible - Second Edition, copyright © 1994.)

Crusaders, 2 Romeland Hill, ST ALBANS, Herts, AL3 4ET. Tel: (01727) 855422.
email@crusaders.org.uk

Contents

The Jigsaw Project has been designed to help you communicate key Christian truths to youngsters growing up in a variety of different social, cultural and family situations.

Introduction

Jigsaw 3 contains 36 <u>more</u> short, straightforward and easy-to-prepare teaching outlines to fit into a club programme. The material is particularly geared to outreach work with youngsters between the ages of 7 and 13... but you could also use it as a basis for teaching in other groups.

Each session outline follows the same pattern:-

BIBLE BASE
- the key passage <u>or</u> verses! (Section headings are taken from the *New Century Version*.)

WE WANT OUR YOUNGSTERS TO...
- the teaching points to bring out of the session;

LEAD-IN*
- an activity to 'set the scene';

HOW TO START*
- a framework to help you teach the main points - please see **Guidelines 1** for more help with this!

ACTIVITIES*
- a choice of <u>TWO</u> activities which link in with or build on the theme - although they appear at the end of the outline, it may sometimes be best to run them before your main teaching;

KEY VERSE
- please see **Guidelines 2** for more help with this!

A PAGE FOR YOUR OWN NOTES WHICH MAY BE HELPFUL...

(* Anything which appears between the symbols ➤ ◀ will need to be done in advance!)

● **YOU can go through the themes in any order, but the sessions within a theme do tend to follow on from each other;**

● **YOU can keep the sessions together in this book... <u>or</u> tear them out along the perforated lines, give them to your co-leaders to prepare, then keep them in a folder afterwards;**

● **YOU will need to select and adapt the material according to the interests of the youngsters in your group;**

and, most importantly,

● **YOU will always need to pray for God's guidance and direction as you prepare to lead each session!**

1. Developing HOW TO START

From the basic framework in each HOW TO START section, you can:

Guidelines

A. **Tell the rest of the story from a Bible story book...** It's worth investing in one which goes through the whole Bible, such as *The Lion Children's Bible* (Lion), *The Lion Storyteller Bible* (Lion) or *The Children's Illustrated Bible* (Dorling Kindersley);

B. **Prepare to re-tell the whole story <u>or</u> present the message in your own words.**

When you are speaking...

- ✔ **practise beforehand.** Be familiar with what you are going to say: it always sounds 'flat' if you read straight from a book <u>or</u> your notes, and it makes eye-contact impossible!
- ✔ **vary the tone and pace of your voice** to go with what you are saying;
- ✔ **introduce different voice types,** (eg for men, women, children, older people etc), <u>but only if you can do them well</u>!

But remember... don't just talk!

Many youngsters find it difficult to learn when they only listen, so:

* ***add visuals***: there are specific suggestions in many sessions - but you can also try them in others! Possibilities include:
   - ○ performing a **drama** for your youngsters to watch;
   - ○ showing a **video**;
   - ○ showing **OHP pictures** - draw your own or trace them from a book;
   - ○ showing **comic strip-style stories** - even simple pin people can be expressive!
   - ○ moving figures and scenes on **metal** or **flannelboard**;
   - ○ using **puppets**;
   - ○ showing **artefacts** ...and so on.

* ***get your youngsters to be as active as possible!*** Again, there are specific suggestions in some sessions. Possibilities include:
   - ○ **discussion** - talk together about feelings, reactions and opinions, (eg how do you think he/she feels? What do you think he/she should do now? What do you think is going to happen next? What do you think about ...? and so on);
   - ○ **art** - have your youngsters sketch the action <u>or</u> the expressions on someone's face as you tell a story;
   - ○ **drama** - have your youngsters act out <u>or</u> mime the action as you tell it   ...and so on.

C. **Occasionally use the passage straight from the Bible...** but only if you check first that it does not contain words and ideas which will be lost on your youngsters! And make sure that you use a good clear, modern version such as the Contemporary English, Good News or New Century versions.

And during your whole programme, always aim to:

- ✔ **be well-prepared...**
- ✔ **keep it fast-moving...** disruption is more likely if your youngsters get bored!
- ✔ **make it varied...** try different ideas and approaches!
- ✔ **let your youngsters know what is expected from them...** it's good to involve them in setting the boundaries <u>right at the outset</u>, (eg 'only one person talks at a time', 'we respect what others do and say', etc). You may have to negotiate, (eg in setting a time limit for the teaching slot - and not overrunning!)
- ✔ **be confident!** After all, if God is with us, we don't need to feel anxious... (*2 Timothy 1:7*)!

2. Helping Youngsters learn a KEY VERSE

Preparation:
* ***Think about how much your youngsters can cope with!***
  If a verse looks too long, don't be afraid to
  ◆ select a key phrase instead of the whole verse...
  ◆ ...or teach it over a number of sessions.

* ***Look at different versions of the Bible:*** we have quoted
  the New Century Version here, but you may prefer to use the
  Contemporary English, Good News or International Children's Bible.

Guidelines

To teach it, try:
○ **putting pictures in place of words**, eg for 'be';

○ **cutting the words into shapes**, eg
  ◆ clothes to hang on a line,
  ◆ weights and a punch bag for a verse about God's strength!
  ◆ footballs or beach balls for a happy verse ...and so on.

○ **writing the words on balloons**.

○ **developing a good rhythm**, eg
  Stand your GROUND
  And you will SEE
  What the Lord CAN DO! Exodus 14:13 (Good News)

○ **singing the verse** to a well-known tune - or make up your own tune!

○ **saying the verse in different voices**, eg whisper, shout, fast, slow motion ...and so on.

○ **adding actions** to the words.

○ **having a team game** with a newspaper - see which team can be the first to make the verse from words and letters in the newspaper!

○ **having a team relay** - cut a copy of the verse into a number of pieces for each team, and place them on a chair or table. Have youngsters run and fetch a piece at a time. See which team is the first to piece together the verse.

○ **asking your youngsters** to come up with ways of learning it!

To help your youngsters learn it, try:
✔ **making sure they understand** its relevance to them!

✔ **reading** the verse through yourself first;
  ➡ then **have your youngsters say it all together**;
  ➡ **repeat** the verse through several times before removing words <u>or</u> adding actions or voices;
  ➡ **including** the verse **in the story**;
  ➡ **reviewing** the verse at different points in the programme;
  ➡ **following up with a take home sheet**, as appropriate.

I have hidden your word in my heart that I might not sin against you...
Psalm 119:11

3. Working with Youngsters in 1990's Britain

○ Be open about what you do and believe as a Christian.

○ Know about the faiths of the youngsters in your group. Also, be aware of things which could cause embarrassment and offence:

  ! never put Bibles, any Bible verses you have written out or songbooks on the floor - some youngsters will think that you have no respect for God or for His Word;

  ! don't insist that someone reads out loud from the Bible, prays out loud or takes part in a dramatisation of a Bible story;

  ! if you are making something with a Bible verse written on it, don't insist that the youngsters take it home;

  ! if you are having food or cooking as an activity, make sure that you cater for everyone, (eg pork is forbidden to youngsters from a Muslim background).

○ Make sure that any pictures or artefacts are multi-cultural.

○ **Support the way the youngsters are being brought up as far as possible.** Try to visit them at home. Every now and then, organise an activity which involves the parents.

○ **Be aware of the family situations of your youngsters.** Avoid talking as if everyone comes from one particular family type, (eg has both parents living at home).

○ **Enjoy the fact that your youngsters come from different backgrounds.** It's really interesting to compare and contrast traditions. Don't feel threatened if youngsters speak in their own language (but it is helpful if you can learn to pick up when they start swearing!)

○ **Be sensitive to youngsters who have difficulties with reading and writing.** Never force anyone to read out loud. Where reading is essential, try to pair non-readers with someone who can read.

○ **Deal decisively with any discriminatory comments and behaviour.** You may also need to watch out for this as the youngsters arrive and leave the premises. Help the youngsters concerned understand why this is not right.

○ **Keep going!** Even when it gets tough, remember that God _is_ at work in the lives of your youngsters:

My dear friends, stand firm and don't be shaken.
Always keep busy working for the Lord.
You know that everything you do for Him is worthwhile.

1 Corinthians 15:58

Checklist

☐ ....
☐ ....
☐ ....
☐ ....
☐ ....
☐ ....

Date ....

Planning Notes

Things to remember for next time...

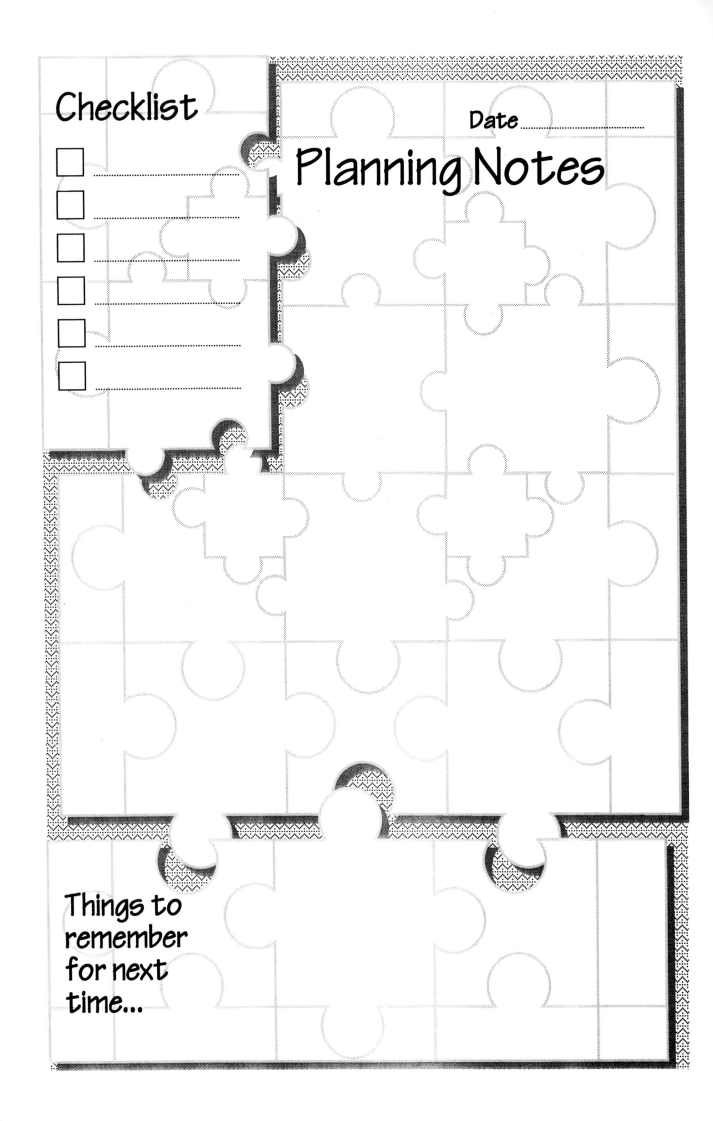

TITLE: God's Perfect World

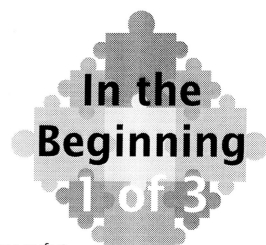

BIBLE BASE: **Genesis 2:4-25** (The First People)

WE WANT OUR YOUNGSTERS TO...

... **see that God created a perfect and beautiful world;**

... **appreciate how important and special they are in God's eyes.**

LEAD-IN: Have a competition to see who can draw a perfect circle free-hand! Talk together about this and about what is meant by perfection. Then ask your youngsters if they can think of anything that is perfect...

HOW TO START:

◆ Begin: *When God made the world, He made a <u>perfect</u> world. The trees, flowers, animals, fish, birds, insects... they were <u>all</u> beautiful and <u>all</u> perfect! And the man and woman God made were given the very special honour of looking after the whole world...*

◆ Ask your youngsters to say which places, animals etc they think are most beautiful;

◆ Say that you are going to show your youngsters some of the most beautiful things that God has ever made... and pass round a mirror!

◆ Go on to talk briefly about how special we are to God.

ACTIVITIES:

1. Conservation Project

Ask: **how can <u>we</u> look after God's world?** Channel your youngsters' interests and energy into a suitable project (eg a campaign to stop people throwing litter, clearing up a (small!) area close by etc).

2. 'God's Beautiful World' Mural

As a whole group, collect together pictures of beautiful things made by God <u>and/or</u> real objects (eg wood, leaves, pebbles etc). Also, have your youngsters draw pictures of themselves <u>or</u> make hand prints (which can be cut out and coloured with paints in accurate skin tones) <u>or</u> take instant polaroid photos of each other. Attach everything to a large piece of paper <u>or</u> cloth <u>or</u> board. Add the words 'God's Beautiful World' and some verses from *Psalm 8* if you wish.

KEY VERSE: *Praise God because he is great! (...) What he does is perfect.*
Deuteronomy 32:3 & 4

Checklist

- ☐ ....
- ☐ ....
- ☐ ....
- ☐ ....
- ☐ ....
- ☐ ....

Date ....

Planning Notes

Things to remember for next time...

TITLE: Forbidden Fruit

BIBLE BASE: Genesis 3:1-24 (The Beginning of Sin)

WE WANT OUR YOUNGSTERS TO...

... **understand that God's perfect world was spoilt when people disobeyed God (- we call this sin);**

... **know that sin was dealt with once and for all by Jesus.**

LEAD-IN: ➤ In advance, seal up a large, <u>empty</u> box. Add a 'no entry' sign, in symbol <u>and/or</u> words. ◄ Show the box and make sure that your youngsters understand the 'no entry' sign! Now ask who would like to open it... Let the suspense about what is in the box build up! Then ask: **why do you want to look inside the box, even though it says that we should not?! Why do we sometimes want to do things we are told not to?** Talk together about specific examples of this which are relevant to your youngsters.

HOW TO START: ◆ Begin: *There was so much for Adam and Eve to enjoy in the beautiful and perfect garden God had made for them! There were so many lovely places to explore! There were so many new plants, animals, birds and insects to find! And all the delicious fruits and foods you can imagine! There was just one thing God asked them not to do...*

◆ Explain that God says 'no' to some things to stop us and other people from being hurt - use real life examples (relevant to your youngsters) to show how sin hurts people;

◆ State clearly that Jesus sorted sin out once and for all when He died on the cross... And develop this, as appropriate to your youngsters..

ACTIVITIES: **1. Drama**

Ask your youngsters to get into small groups. Ask each group to act out a really good and happy situation (eg a birthday party, a game etc). Then stop the action. Now ask each group to act out what happens in that situation when someone does something selfish... be ready with ideas! Have an opportunity to see and talk about both parts of each group's drama. Highlight the damage done by one person doing wrong! Help your youngsters see that we are all guilty of doing things like this - otherwise they may focus on the wrong things others have done to them! Lead into prayer, as appropriate to your group.

2. Blot!

Give each youngster a small, clean piece of paper. Then add a blot of ink <u>or</u> dye to each one. Liken this to what happened to God's perfect world when Adam and Eve wanted their own way. Ask your youngsters how to make the paper perfectly clean again... it's impossible! Now get them to disguise their ink blot by drawing a picture around it. Have an opportunity to see everyone's ideas. Talk about how we try to 'cover up' things which we do wrong (eg by hiding something we've broken, by blaming others etc). Point out that the ink blot is still there! Liken this to the things which we do wrong. Go on to say that only being forgiven by God will make us clean again! Lead into prayer, as appropriate to your group.

KEY VERSE: *[Christ] died to defeat the power of sin once - enough for all time.* Romans 6:10

Checklist

☐ ....

☐ ....

☐ ....

☐ ....

☐ ....

☐ ....

Date ....

Planning Notes

Things to remember for next time...

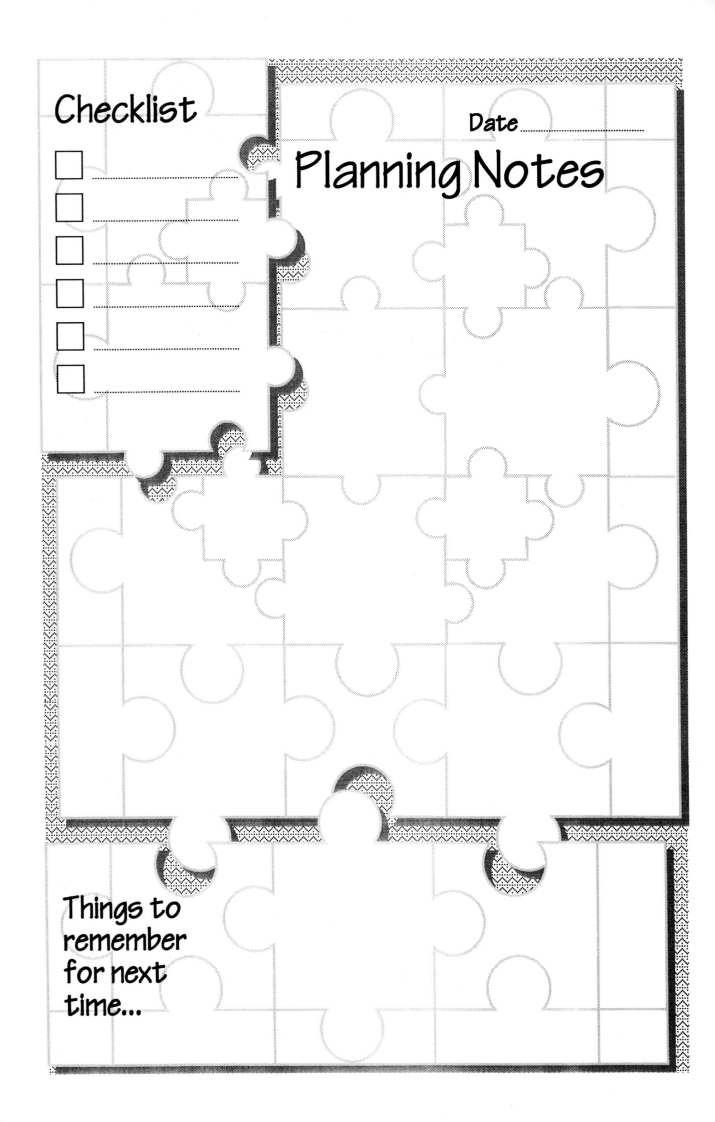

TITLE: A Jealous Brother

BIBLE BASE: **Genesis 4:1-16** (The First Family)

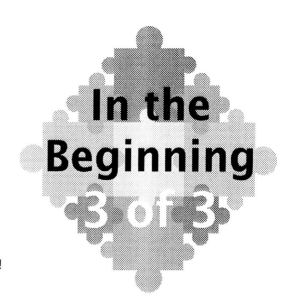

WE WANT OUR YOUNGSTERS TO...

... **think about the harm jealousy causes in their own lives - and take action to curb it;**

... **think about what causes arguments between them and their brothers and/or sisters - and take action to prevent them!**

LEAD-IN: Bring in three pieces of coloured card <u>or</u> cloth: one red, one green and one gold. For each one, ask: **what does the colour make you think of?** Home in on: red = love, anger, danger, blood; green = growing, living, jealousy; gold = rich, a king/queen, the best!

HOW TO START:
◆ Give each youngster three small pieces of paper <u>or</u> cloth: one red, one green and one gold. As you tell the story, ask them to hold up the colour which comes into their mind, (eg red for Cain's anger when his gift is rejected).

◆ Begin: *Have you ever felt jealous of someone - perhaps because someone has something you don't have? Or maybe because someone can do something you can't do? Cain was very jealous <u>and</u> angry when he took a gift to God...*

ACTIVITIES: **1. Do the Best Thing!**

➤ In advance, think up one or two situations which involve jealousy <u>and/or</u> arguments between brothers and sisters - make sure that they are relevant to your youngsters! ◄ Ask for volunteers to come and begin to act out the situation. Stop the action at an appropriate point and ask the rest of your group: **what should he/she do next?** Weigh up the different suggestions. Have a vote. Then ask your volunteers to continue to act, following this advice.

2. A Gift for God

Talk together about why we give gifts to people... Then consider giving a gift to God (but make sure that your youngsters know that we give gifts to God to show Him we love Him, not to earn His approval!). <u>Either</u> in small groups <u>or</u> altogether, prepare something appropriate (eg a song, picture, poem, dance; doing something for someone in need etc). Then 'give the gift'!

KEY VERSE: *Try to learn what pleases the Lord.* Ephesians 5:10

Checklist

☐ ....
☐ ....
☐ ....
☐ ....
☐ ....
☐ ....

Date ....

Planning Notes

Things to remember for next time...

TITLE: The Hidden Baby

Moses
1 of 6

BIBLE BASE: **Exodus 1:1-2:10** (*from* Jacob's Family Grows Strong *to* Baby Moses)

WE WANT OUR YOUNGSTERS TO...

... **see God at work 'behind the scenes';**

... **understand that God has plans for our lives which start when we are born.**

LEAD-IN: Have a game of 'Hunt the Baby'!
➤ In advance, hide a packet of Jelly Babies or baby shapes cut out of paper around your meeting room or outdoors. ◀ Give any youngsters who find a 'baby' a clean Jelly Baby or other sweet.

HOW TO START: ◆ Talk together about your youngsters' experiences of looking after babies. Ask: **what do babies need? Who provides these things?** Perhaps make a list as you go along, large enough for everyone to see.

◆ Begin: *When Baby Moses was born, his own family could not care for him for very long. His family were slaves in a country called Egypt. The new king of Egypt had given the terrible order that all baby boys born to slave families should be killed! Moses' mum hid him for three months, but she knew that someone would find him soon. Then she had an idea...*

◆ Help your youngsters see how God provided all that Baby Moses needed.

◆ Say that God already had special plans for Baby Moses - just as He has for each one of us!

ACTIVITIES:

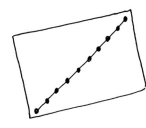

1. Time Line

➤ In advance, draw a diagonal line across a piece of A4 paper. Roughly mark off years up to ten (or the age of your oldest youngster!). Then make copies - enough for one each. ◀ Help your youngsters mark on their 'time line' things which have happened to them (eg starting school, moving house etc) - they could do this in pictures and/or words. Be ready to pick up any difficult issues and memories which arise... Talk with them sensitively about their 'time lines' - help them see how God has been looking out for them all along. If appropriate:

• have your youngsters show their 'time lines' to each other in a small group;
• have them add the KEY VERSE.

2. God's Plans - My Part

Ask your youngsters to get into groups of about six with a leader. Ask one person from each group to lie down on the floor. Have the rest of the group draw round him/her with chalk. Now ask: **how can we use the different parts of us to help bring about God's plans?** Get the groups to write their ideas on the body shape (eg lips to say good things to others; hands to help others etc). Have an opportunity to see each group's body shape. Then pray together!

KEY VERSE: *I have good plans for you (...) I will give you hope and a good future.*
Jeremiah 29:11

Checklist

☐ ....

☐ ....

☐ ....

☐ ....

☐ ....

☐ ....

Date ....

Planning Notes

Things to
remember
for next
time...

TITLE: The Runaway Prince

BIBLE BASE: **Exodus 2:11-23** (Moses Tries to Help & Moses in Midian)

WE WANT OUR YOUNGSTERS TO...

... know that God cares about people suffering;

... see that violence causes more problems than it solves!

LEAD-IN: Play a variation of 'Duck, duck, goose'! Have your youngsters sit in a large circle facing inwards. Walk round the outside of the circle, tapping each youngster on the shoulder and saying his/her name as you do. After a while, call one of your youngsters 'Moses'! He/she has to chase you round the circle: you both aim to be the first one to sit in 'Moses' empty space - the one who isn't, begins walking round the circle... and so on. Lead in by saying that, one day, Moses really did have to run...!

HOW TO START:
◆ Have a small group of youngsters mime the action to the rest of your group as you tell the story.
◆ Begin: ***Moses stretched and yawned - just another ordinary day! He had no idea that, after today, nothing would ever be the same again...***
◆ Talk together about Moses killing the Egyptian. Ask: **what could he have done differently?**

ACTIVITIES: **1. Two Wrongs Never Make a Right!**

➤ In advance, draw a simple picture of one stick figure hitting another stick figure. The image should fill about 1/4 of an A4 sheet. <u>Either</u> make copies - enough for one between four - <u>or</u> draw pictures of several other situations which could get worse if the 'victim' retaliated (eg calling names, spoiling games etc). ◄ Ask your youngsters to get into small groups with a leader. Ask each group to look at the picture and talk about what might happen next - then draw it. Have them talk about the consequences of that action, then draw it... and so on. Bring out clearly how the situation escalates! Help your youngsters come up with realistic and Biblical steps to avoid this kind of situation. <u>But be sensitive</u> - some youngsters will have been taught to hit back! Also, make sure that you are not advocating passive resistance to abuse. Pray about any real-life situations mentioned by your youngsters.

2. Code of Behaviour

If fighting is sometimes a problem in your group, help your youngsters work out a 'Code of Behaviour' to help deal with it. Perhaps have your youngsters sign it to show that they agree with it! Have the 'Code' easily visible over the coming weeks - and use it!

KEY VERSE: *Live in peace with each other.* 1 Thessalonians 5:13

Checklist

☐ ....
☐ ....
☐ ....
☐ ....
☐ ....
☐ ....

Date ....

Planning Notes

Things to remember for next time...

TITLE: The Reluctant Leader

Moses
3 of 6

BIBLE BASE: Exodus 3:1-4:17 (*from* The Burning Bush *to* Proof for Moses)

WE WANT OUR YOUNGSTERS TO...

... begin to understand that God is Holy;

... understand that when God asks us to do something, He will give us all that we need to do it well!

LEAD-IN: ➤ In advance, think of about six jobs <u>or</u> positions which involve leadership, (eg teacher, parent etc). Write each one out large on a separate piece of paper. ◄ Spread them all out, face down. Now ask for a volunteer. Let him/her choose a piece of paper. Then ask him/her to give three clues about the person on it - get everyone else to guess who it is! Do the same with the other jobs. Finally, show all the pieces of paper. Ask: **what do these jobs have in common?** Talk briefly about what it means to be a leader.

HOW TO START: ◆ ➤ In advance, rehearse the story as a conversation between Moses and a friend, eg:
Friend: *Moses, what's happened? You look as if you've had a shock!*
Moses: *I still can't quite believe it! I was just minding the sheep, as usual, when I noticed the most amazing thing...* ◄
When you 'perform' it, involve your youngsters in asking questions too!
◆ Ask: **why do you think God told Moses to take off his sandals?** Use your youngsters' answers in a very simple explanation of God's holiness.
◆ Ask: **why do you think Moses made so many excuses? What would you have said?** Talk simply about how God equips us for the jobs He gives us.

ACTIVITIES: **1. Grow your Leaders!**

It's never too soon to start looking for and developing leadership potential in your youngsters! Think of simple things they can be responsible for in your club, (eg helping keep a register, helping with younger children, teaching a new game <u>or</u> a craft activity etc). Ask your youngsters to get into small groups and plan something. Be on hand to offer advice, but be willing to stand back and let them try (even if they might not do things the way you would!). Pray specifically for your youngsters in what they take on. And make this an ongoing part of your programme!

2. Excuses, Excuses...

➤ In advance, think of three or four tasks your youngsters would probably be asked to do (eg looking after a younger brother or sister, doing the washing-up etc). ◄ Ask your youngsters to get into pairs or threes. Read out the first task and ask your youngsters to come up with a good reason not to do it - keep it fun at this stage! Hear and enjoy a few excuses before moving onto the next task each time. Use this as a springboard for a more serious discussion on the excuses we really make for not doing what others ask us to do. If appropriate, extend this to think about the excuses we make to God. Then pray!

KEY VERSE: *Who is like you, wonderful in holiness?* Exodus 15:11 (GNB)

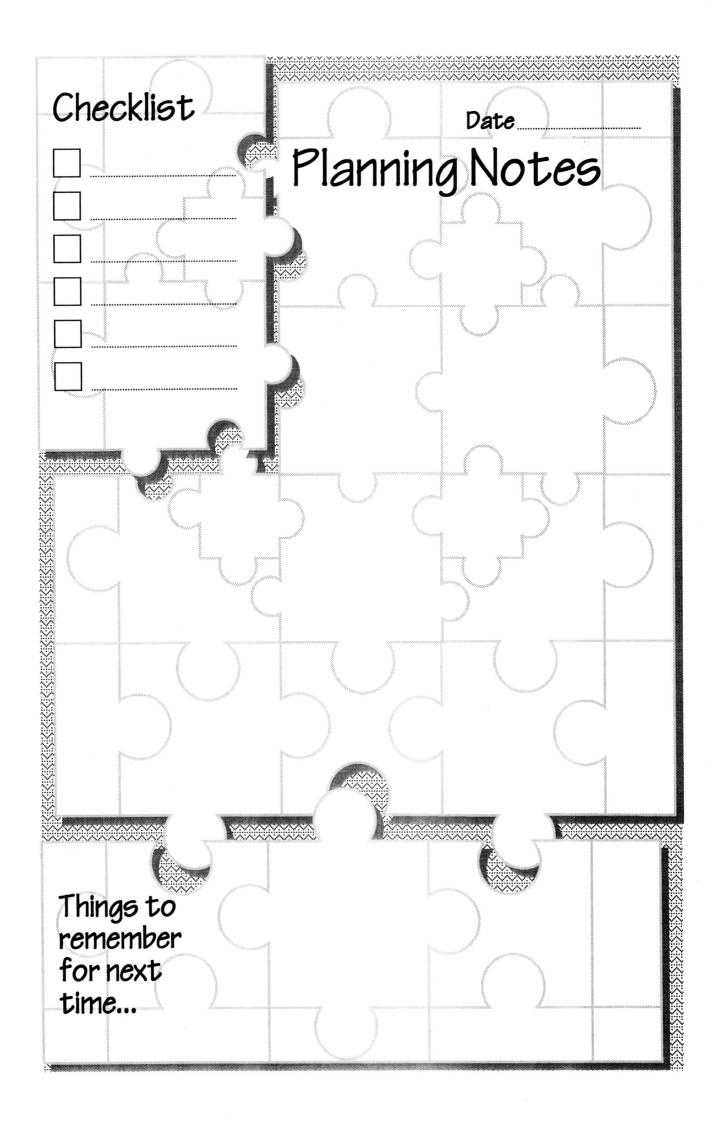

Checklist

☐ ....
☐ ....
☐ ....
☐ ....
☐ ....
☐ ....

Date ....

Planning Notes

Things to remember for next time...

TITLE: **The Slaves'
Spokesperson**

Moses

4 of 6

BIBLE BASE: **Exodus 7:1-10:29** (*from* God
Repeats His Call to Moses *to*
The Darkness)

WE WANT OUR YOUNGSTERS TO...
    ... **see that God is more powerful
than the most powerful people;**
    ... **think about whether they 'harden
their hearts' against God.**

LEAD-IN: Organise a test of strength (eg arm <u>or</u> finger wrestling etc). Find out who is
the champion! Ask him/her: **how does it feel to be the most powerful?** Talk
briefly about different kinds of power...

HOW TO START: ◆ Ask your youngsters to get into eight groups. Write the eight plagues out
on separate pieces of paper and give one to each group. Ask each group to
create a sound effect <u>or</u> action <u>or</u> large picture symbol to go with its
plague... Have each group 'perform' as its plague appears in the story!
◆ Begin: *Was Moses dreaming? One day he was out in the hills caring for
his flocks - and the next he was standing before the most powerful man
in all Egypt...!*
◆ Focus on how the king reacted. Use this to help your youngsters think
about how we can ignore God...

ACTIVITIES: **1. Faces**

➤ In advance, cut face shapes out of paper <u>or</u> card. ◄ Give one to each
youngster. Ask them to think of someone in the story (eg the king, a person
who has seen the blood in the Nile, a person with boils... etc). Be ready with
ideas! Now ask them to draw and/or paint that person's face. Have an
opportunity to see and enjoy everyone's 'faces'.

2. Breakdown!

➤ In advance, collect together a number of large, empty boxes. ◄ Also, make
lots of light balls by scrunching up and taping newspaper. Stack the boxes to
make a wall. Ask your youngsters to get into two teams - A and B. Have team
A stand in front of the wall to protect it (but they are not allowed to touch <u>or</u>
repair it), whilst team B stands behind a line and tries to destroy the wall by
throwing the paper balls at it! Allow one minute for this, then swap over. The
team which destroys most of the wall, wins! As appropriate, talk about
attitudes and actions which are like putting up a wall against God, (eg doing
what I want, not forgiving others, following friends and not God etc).
Challenge your youngsters about them. Perhaps write them on paper, stick
them to the boxes and play the game again!

KEY VERSE: *Today listen to what he says. Do not be stubborn as in the past when you
turned against God.* Hebrews 3:15

Checklist

☐ ....

☐ ....

☐ ....

☐ ....

☐ ....

☐ ....

Date ....

Planning Notes

Things to remember for next time...

TITLE: Free at Last!

BIBLE BASE: **Exodus 11:1-13:2** (The Death of the Firstborn **&** Israel Leaves Egypt)

WE WANT OUR YOUNGSTERS TO...
   ... hear that Jesus' death brings us life forever! (ie the link between the Passover Lamb and Jesus.)

LEAD-IN: Give everyone a small piece of card. Have everyone put their fingerprint on it and then add their name. Help your youngsters turn this into a badge, perhaps by sticking a small safety pin on the back. Have everyone wear their badges! Talk about other forms of identification and why we have them. Perhaps also bring a passport or ID card to show. Ask your youngsters to listen for a sign which marked out God's people...

HOW TO START:
◆ Begin: *Blood, boils, darkness, locusts, frogs... All these signs from God and the king still refused to listen! God wanted the king to free his people, who were being kept as slaves. "Nobody tells me what to do!" thought the king to himself. Then God spoke to Moses again about another plague... and this one was more terrible than all the rest...*
◆ Show a cross. Ask: **what is this a sign for?** See if your youngsters spot any links between this and the blood on the doorposts...
◆ Remind them that a lamb died to save a life. Say simply and clearly that this is like Jesus - He died to give us life forever.

ACTIVITIES: **1. Quiz**

➤ In advance, think of some different signs and symbols, (eg road signs, symbols on maps, well-known brand logos etc) - include a cross. Draw them out on paper and number them. Tack them around the wall before your youngsters arrive. ◄ Have your youngsters go round in pairs and try to guess what each sign means. Give prizes, as appropriate. Reinforce the meaning of the cross.

2. Lifesaver

Show a video in which someone dies or risks his/her life to save someone else (eg 'the Lion King'). Make a link with the teaching content, as appropriate.

KEY VERSE: *[Jesus said:] "The good shepherd gives his life for the sheep."* John 10:11

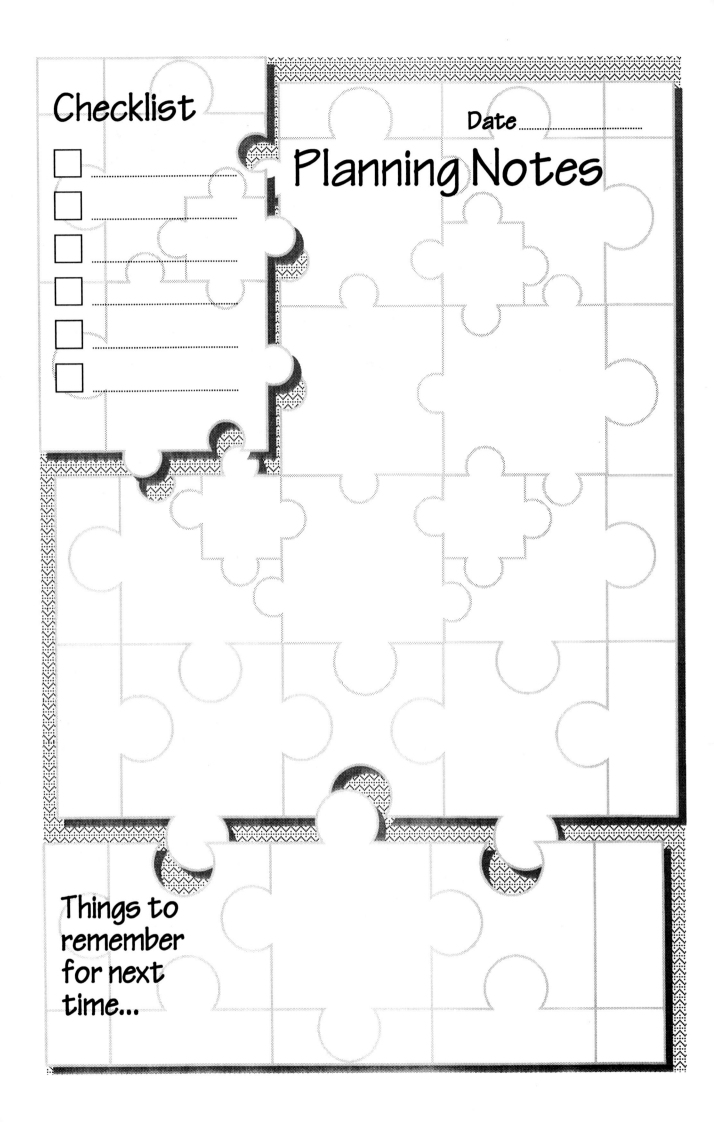

Checklist

☐ ....
☐ ....
☐ ....
☐ ....
☐ ....
☐ ....

Date ....

Planning Notes

Things to remember for next time...

TITLE: **A Reason to Sing**

BIBLE BASE: **Exodus 14:1-15:18** (*from* The Way Out of Egypt *to* The Song of Moses)

WE WANT OUR YOUNGSTERS TO...

... **see that God has power over the forces of nature;**

... **recognise that God protected His people - and ask Him for protection.**

LEAD-IN:

➤ In advance, get together one or two things you have power over, ie you can make them do what you want them to do, (eg a radio controlled toy etc). ◄ Show and play with the things, as appropriate. Ask your youngsters for other examples of things they have power over. Then talk about things they have no power over (eg the weather!).

HOW TO START:

◆ As you tell the story, bring out clearly the points where the people had no power... and then how God stepped in with His amazing power!

◆ Begin: *"God is absolutely amazing!" Moses thought to himself. As the people sat down to rest that evening, everybody was talking about what God had done. "Nobody else could have done that, Lord," said Moses, "You are the only One who can make amazing things happen...!"*

◆ Ask: **what did the people learn about God that day?** Bring out both God's power and His protection.

◆ As appropriate, pray together for protection for your youngsters and for others known to them.

ACTIVITIES:

1. Helping Hands

➤ In advance, get together the equipment and ingredients for some everyday activities (eg cleaning teeth, drinking, eating etc). ◄ Now ask your youngsters to get into pairs (A and B), with A standing behind B. B puts his/her arms behind his/her back and cannot use them: A puts his/her arms forward under B's arms, ready to use. Now have A give B a drink, clean B's teeth etc! Swap over if you have time! Ask A: **how did it feel to have power over your partner?** As appropriate, develop this into a discussion of the power we have over others, how we use it... and how it compares to God's power.

2. Sharks and Swimmers

You will need a lot of space! Mark out about four 'rocks' (eg an area encircled by chairs). Choose some leaders (or youngsters) to be 'sharks' and say that everyone else is a 'swimmer'! Have all the 'swimmers' move around the room. Shout out different strokes (ie breast stroke, back stroke etc) for the 'swimmers' to do, changing them frequently! When you shout out 'shark!', 'swimmers' must 'swim' to a 'rock' for safety: anybody caught by a 'shark' before reaching a 'rock' becomes a 'shark' for the rest of the game! Continue until you have just one 'swimmer' left - the winner! As appropriate, make links with how we can run to God, our Rock, for protection.

KEY VERSE: *My God is the rock of my protection.* Psalm 94:22

Checklist

☐ ....

☐ ....

☐ ....

☐ ....

☐ ....

☐ ....

Date ....

Planning Notes

Things to
remember
for next
time...

TITLE: On the Run!

BIBLE BASE: **Jonah 1:1-3** (God Calls and
Jonah Runs)

WE WANT OUR YOUNGSTERS TO...

... understand that God is loving
and merciful;
... consider that it is not always easy
to do the right thing...

LEAD-IN: Ask your youngsters to get into two teams. Set
up an obstacle course using chairs, tables, benches
etc (but make sure that none of the obstacles presents
a danger!). Have the two teams race each other over the obstacle course.
Award small prizes to the quickest team, if you wish. Then have two leaders
do the race - but one of them ignores all the obstacles and just runs the race!
Ask everyone what they think of this! Point out that it was much easier to
break the rules than do the race properly...

HOW TO START: ◆ Begin: *Nineveh city was wicked - and I mean wicked! For many years,
the people who lived in Nineveh had ignored God. All sorts of horrible,
evil things went on in the city. And God saw everything... "This cannot
go on!" He thought. "Now, who can I get to go and warn them? I know
just the person..."*
◆ Ask: **how would you have felt if you were Jonah? Why do you think
Jonah chose to disobey God and do something else instead?**

ACTIVITIES: **1. Real Obstacles**

Ask your youngsters to tell you about the things they <u>least</u> like doing. Make a
list of them as you go along. Then talk together about what would happen if
we never did any of those things! Perhaps have your youngsters draw a
cartoon to go with one of them (eg the situation if we never tidied up...! etc).
Bring out the idea that it is not always easy to do the right thing - but it's
always worth it in the end. As appropriate, ask your youngsters to identify a
right thing they have been avoiding - will they go and do it? Then pray!

2. Questionnaire

➤ In advance, devise your own questionnaire on dilemmas which are relevant
to the lives of your youngsters, eg 'At school you see some of your friends
bullying a younger child. Do you... a) join in, because friends do things
together? b) walk away and pretend not to notice? c) tell a teacher and risk
losing your friends?' ◄ Have your youngsters choose what they are most
likely to do each time. Then talk together about the situations.

KEY VERSE: *[Jesus said:] "...if you obey my commands, you will remain in my love."*
John 15:10

Checklist

☐ ....
☐ ....
☐ ....
☐ ....
☐ ....
☐ ....

Date ....

Planning Notes

Things to remember for next time...

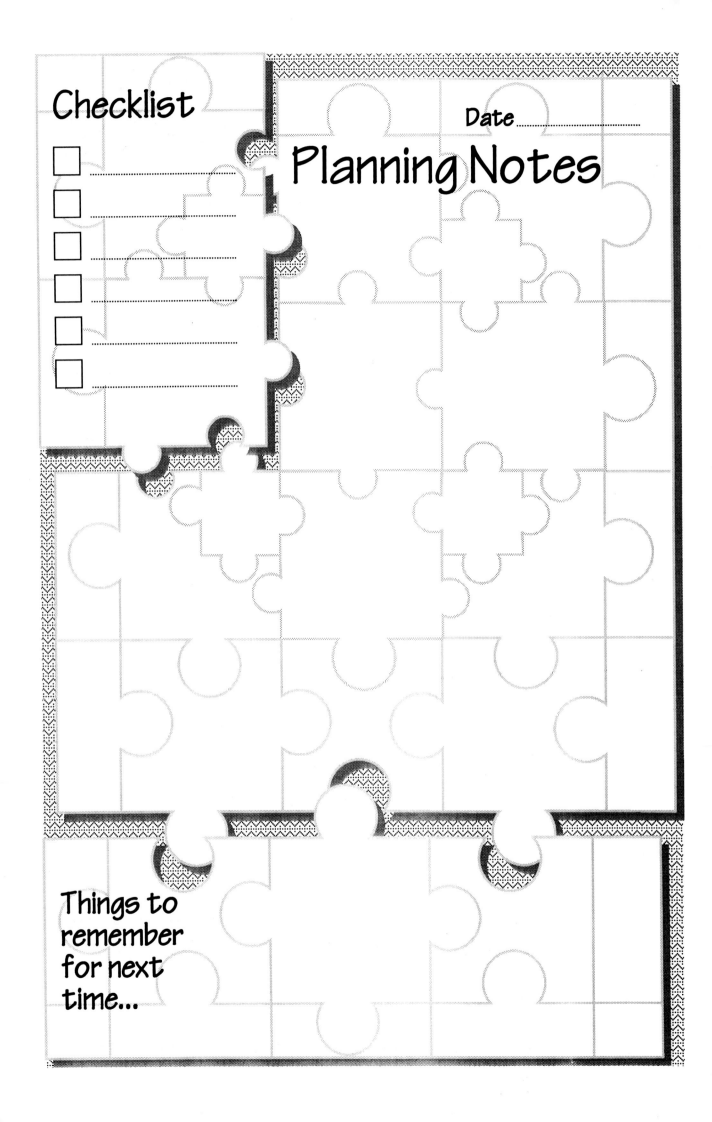

TITLE: Nowhere to Hide!

BIBLE BASE: Jonah 1:4-16 (God Calls and Jonah Runs & Jonah's Punishment)

WE WANT OUR YOUNGSTERS TO...

... understand that we cannot hide from God!

LEAD-IN: Give a youngster or leader a soft ball and ask him/her to stand in the middle of the room. He/she has to 'attack' other youngsters by throwing the ball at their legs. Everyone else can run and jump around to avoid the ball. When someone is hit, they join the youngster or leader as an 'attacker'. Introduce more soft balls into the game if you have them. Continue until everyone is on the 'attacking' team! Point out that, however good people were at running and jumping, nobody could avoid being hit forever...

HOW TO START:
◆ Begin: *As Jonah stepped on board the ship, he felt really pleased with himself. "I am running away from God!" he thought. The ship was about to leave for Spain - Spain is a very long way from Nineveh, where God wanted him to be! There was nothing to stop Jonah now... or was there...?*
◆ Stop the story just after the sailors draw lots and find that Jonah is the cause of the trouble. Ask: **how do you think Jonah must have felt?**
◆ Talk together about how it feels when you are found out for doing something wrong.

ACTIVITIES:

1. Masks

➤ In advance, cut oval shapes about the size of a youngster's face from stiff paper or card - enough for one each. ◀ Have each child make a mask with pens or paints (and any other materials you can provide.) Attach a length of cord or thin elastic to the back of each mask so that it can be worn. Point out that masks hide what we look like, but they do not hide what we are really like inside! As appropriate, talk about how good it is that God knows **all** about us... And pray!

2. Key Verse

➤ In advance, write the words of the KEY VERSE out large on separate pieces of paper. If necessary, do this again in different coloured pens, so that you have enough for each youngster to have a word. Hide the words around your meeting room before everyone arrives. ◀ Now have your youngsters find them all! Lay the words out on a table and put the whole verse together as a group.

KEY VERSE: *Lord, you have examined me and you know all about me.* Psalm 139:1

Checklist

- ☐ ....
- ☐ ....
- ☐ ....
- ☐ ....
- ☐ ....
- ☐ ....

Date ....

Planning Notes

Things to remember for next time...

TITLE: Swallowed Alive!

BIBLE BASE: Jonah 1:17-2:10 (Jonah's Punishment)

WE WANT OUR YOUNGSTERS TO...

... see that God gives people a second chance;

... know that God forgives us completely - He does not remember the things we do wrong (and neither should we!).

LEAD-IN: Have a game of 'Dead and Alive'! Everyone runs round the room and a leader(s) <u>or</u> youngster(s) 'tags'... When a youngster is 'tagged', he/she must stand still with his/her arms outstretched. He/she cannot move until someone else touches both his/her hands - he/she is then 'alive' and can continue playing the game. Point out that 'tagged' youngsters needed someone else to get them out of trouble...

HOW TO START:
◆ Begin: *"Help!" cried Jonah, "help me!" The waves were enormous all around him and he struggled to keep his head above the water. Jonah knew that no man or woman could save him now... But he knew someone who could still come to his rescue...*
◆ Ask: **why do you think Jonah praised and thanked God inside the fish?**

ACTIVITIES:

1. Inside the Fish...

...it must have been dark, smelly and unpleasant! ➤ As a fun way of getting your youngsters to experience what this might have been like, collect together a variety of different objects in advance... perhaps include some things which feel slippery, cold, slimy and horrible! ◄ Ask for two or three volunteers. Blindfold them. Give each object to the volunteers in turn... they must describe the object and try and guess what it is!

2. Stop Running and Hiding!

Talk simply with your youngsters about how we can be like Jonah. Be clear about Jesus wanting to forgive us and forget all that we have done wrong and give us a second chance... Then give each youngster a piece of paper. Ask everyone to draw <u>and/or</u> cut out a large fish shape and draw <u>or</u> write on it (perhaps something they remember they have done wrong, but not owned up to God about). Say that no-one else but God will see this. Pray together. If appropriate, then have your youngsters tear their fish-shapes up. Take the pieces right away as an illustration of the fact that the wrong things have been forgiven and forgotten.

KEY VERSE: *When I was in danger, I called to the Lord and he answered me.* Jonah 2:2

Checklist

☐ ....

☐ ....

☐ ....

☐ ....

☐ ....

☐ ....

Date ....

Planning Notes

Things to remember for next time...

TITLE: The Message

BIBLE BASE: **Jonah 3:1-10** (God Calls and Jonah Obeys)

Jonah
4 of 4

WE WANT OUR YOUNGSTERS TO...

... **know that God is loving and merciful;**

... **understand that God wants us to tell other people about His love and forgiveness - and not keep it to ourselves!**

LEAD-IN:
➤ In advance, tie a shoe to a length of rope.◄ Have your youngsters stand in a circle facing inward. Stand in the middle and swing the rope round at ankle height - your youngsters have to jump the rope as it passes them. If anyone mis-times their jump, the rope will wrap around their legs... Usually, this means that they are OUT, but, to link in with the teaching content, give them another chance...!

HOW TO START:
◆ Begin: *Jonah knew all about second chances! God had saved Jonah from drowning and was giving him a second chance to take the message to the people in Nineveh... Now it was their turn to be given a second chance...*

ACTIVITIES:

1. Pass it On! A

Ask your youngsters to get into two teams. Play some relay games in which something has to be passed from one person to another, eg 'Under and Over': person A passes a ball over his/her head to person B; person B passes it between his/her legs to person C ...and so on. Point out that it was no use a person keeping the ball to him/herself - it had to be passed on. Linking in with the story, go on to say that Jonah knew what it was like to be loved and forgiven by God - now he had to pass the good news on!

2. Pass it On! B

➤ In advance, think of an appropriate way to pass on a message (eg a card, a poster, a letter etc). ◄ Have your youngsters design and make a card or a poster or notepaper, using whatever materials you can provide. Encourage them to add the words: God loves me and He loves you too! Ask your youngsters to pass the message on, either to someone in the group or to a friend or family member outside the group.

KEY VERSE:
So go and make followers of all people in the world (...) Teach them to obey everything I have taught you. Matthew 28:19-20

Checklist

☐ ....

☐ ....

☐ ....

☐ ....

☐ ....

☐ ....

Date ....

Planning Notes

Things to remember for next time...

TITLE: "I am the Bread of Life..."

BIBLE BASE: John 6:25-59 (Jesus, the Bread of Life)

WE WANT OUR YOUNGSTERS TO...

... understand that Jesus brings life and is essential for it;

... learn simply how they can receive this 'bread'.

LEAD-IN: ➤ In advance, get hold of some different types of bread (eg granary, naan, pitta etc). ◄ Hand them round, so that everyone has a little to try. Talk about the different sorts of bread. Find out which ones your youngsters like best. Now ask: **has anyone ever been really hungry? What does it feel like to be really hungry?**

HOW TO START: ◆ Have some bread on show throughout. Using a mixture of questions and answers and short explanations, try to bring out the following points, as appropriate to the youngsters in your group:

- we all need food to keep our bodies alive;
- we also need 'food' to live with God;
- Jesus said, *'I am the bread that gives life'*... this means that He can give us life with God for ever;
- Jesus gives us this special life with God when we ask Him to be our friend, say sorry for the wrong things we have done and follow Him;
- we need to eat several times a day, otherwise we'll get really hungry!
- we also need Jesus in our lives <u>every day</u> if we want to grow in our friendship with Him.

ACTIVITIES: 1. Eat Your Words!

➤ In advance, get hold of some edible letters (eg spaghetti, biscuits, savoury snacks etc). ◄ Have the words LOVE, LIFE, JOY, PEACE and POWER written out large. Ask your youngsters to get into teams of about four. Give each team a plate and some edible letters. See which team is the first to make the words from these letters! Say that Jesus brings us all these things when we ask Him to be our friend and follow Him. Finish by inviting your youngsters to 'eat their words'!

2. **Taste and See**

Open a whole packet of sweets <u>or</u> small cakes in front of your group. Take one out and begin to eat it... say how delicious it is and make lots of appreciative faces and noises! When you have finished, put the packet away and say, "that was really good, wasn't it?!" When the protests have died down (!), point out that we won't know what Jesus, 'the Bread of Life', is like by watching other people share their lives with Him... we won't know how good He is until we ask Him ourselves to be our friend. Then share the sweets <u>or</u> cakes round!

KEY VERSE: *[Jesus said:] "I am the bread that gives life.... Anyone who eats this bread will live for ever."* John 6:35 & 51

Checklist

☐ ....
☐ ....
☐ ....
☐ ....
☐ ....
☐ ....

Date ....

Planning Notes

Things to remember for next time...

TITLE:	**"I am the Light of the World..."**
BIBLE BASE:	**John 1:4-5, 8:12 & 9:1-7** (Jesus is the Light of the World)

WE WANT OUR YOUNGSTERS TO...
> ... understand that Jesus shows us the truth and guides us - if we ask Him to!
> ... learn simply how Jesus can be light in their lives.

LEAD-IN:

➤ In advance, set out some obstacles in the room - boxes, furniture... and leaders! ◄ Then ask your youngsters to each find a partner. Blindfold one in each pair, then have his/her partner guide him/her over the obstacles. Swap round and repeat, if you have time. Ask the youngsters who were blindfolded: **how did you feel? Did you trust your partner to guide you?** Perhaps go on to talk about what your youngsters would be sad **not** to see if they were blind.

HOW TO START:

◆ ➤ In advance, ask some leaders <u>or</u> youngsters to prepare a mime of the miracle in *John 9:1-7.* ◄

◆ Begin: ***One day, when Jesus was walking down the street, He met a man who had been born blind. This man had <u>never</u> seen his family or his friends or... Watch this mime to see what happened next...!***

◆ After the mime, help your youngsters to imagine what it would have been like for the man to see for the first time.

◆ Ask: **what do you think Jesus meant when He said He is** *'the light of the world'?*

◆ Go on to explain that Jesus made blind people see, but also that He helps us 'see' things about God - He shows us what God is like, how we can know Him ourselves and the best way to live!

ACTIVITIES:

1. Discovering God

➤ In advance, write ten simple truths about God on separate pieces of paper (eg God is love, God is kind etc). ◄ Stick them on the walls and furniture before your youngsters arrive. Now get your youngsters into small groups with a leader and a torch! Now turn out the lights and ask your youngsters to go round in their groups, finding all the messages. Then talk together about them.

2. 'Reflection'

Get all your youngsters to stand in a circle. Give everyone a nightlight (ie a candle in a small container). Light one youngster's nightlight and turn out the lights. Go round and light all the nightlights. <u>Alternatively</u>, if your youngsters are reasonably trustworthy, have the first youngster light the second youngster's nightlight, the second light the third and so on. Whichever you choose, finish with a song <u>or</u> a prayer <u>or</u> a short Bible passage <u>or</u> a poem...

Extra: Focus on the problems blind people face today: perhaps invite someone from the 'Royal National Institute for the Blind' <u>or</u> 'Guide Dogs for the Blind' <u>or</u> send for some information and talk together about it. Then pray and perhaps organise a short-term project to help.

KEY VERSE:

[Jesus said:] "I am the light of the world. The person who follows me will (...) have the light that gives life." John 8:12

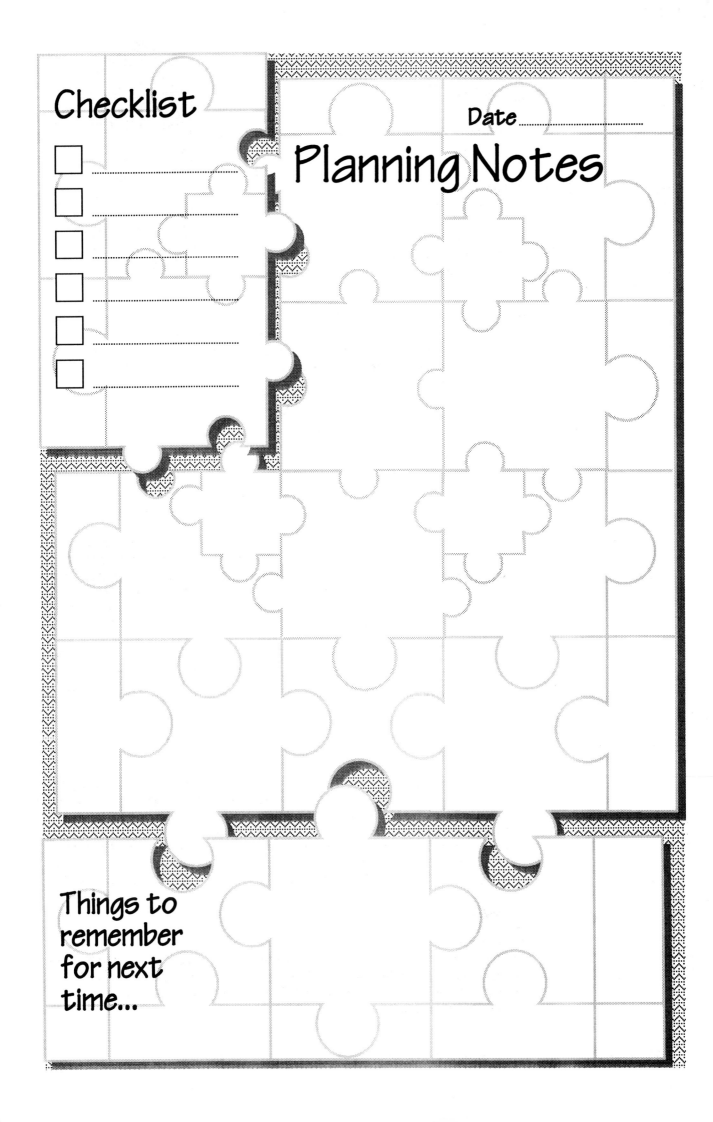

Checklist

- ☐
- ☐
- ☐
- ☐
- ☐
- ☐

Date _____

Planning Notes

Things to remember for next time...

TITLE: "I am the Gate for the Sheep..."

BIBLE BASE: John 10:7-15 (Jesus is the Good Shepherd)

WE WANT OUR YOUNGSTERS TO...
- ... understand that Jesus is the way into God's presence;
- ... be assured that He knows and loves each one of them personally.

LEAD-IN: ➤ In advance, think of about five 'ways in' (eg gate, door, turnstile etc). Have leaders or youngsters work out some actions to show each one (eg four people moving round in a cross-shape could be a revolving door!). ◄ Show each mime and have the youngsters guess what it is! For each one, ask: **what could this be a way into?**

HOW TO START:
- ◆ Draw a large 'C' on a board or poster-sized paper.
- ◆ Ask: **what could this be?** Get a number of answers before saying that it is a sheepfold!
- ◆ Sketch in stone walls as you explain: *wolves and thieves are a danger to sheep in the country where Jesus lived. At night, shepherds keep their sheep in a sheepfold, which is a C-shape made of stones. Shepherds know and care for each of the sheep in their flock. To keep them safe, shepherds lay across the gap in the sheepfold wall all night long to make a gate. They are ready to risk their lives to keep their sheep safe against wolves or thieves!*
- ◆ Continue drawing as you say: *Jesus said we are like sheep. He said He is like a gate for the sheep - a gate to God! Once we have come to God through Jesus, then nothing and nobody can take us away from God again!*

ACTIVITIES:

1. Sheep and Wolves

Mark out a C-shaped 'sheepfold' with rope or chalk. Spread 'food' (eg paper, dried peas etc) all around your meeting room. Choose a leader or youngster to be a 'wolf' and you be the 'shepherd' - everyone else is a 'sheep'! Begin with all the 'sheep grazing', ie picking up the scattered 'food'! When the 'wolf' attacks, the 'sheep' run into the 'fold' and you act as the 'gate' to keep the 'sheep' safe. If the 'wolf' touches a 'sheep' on the way to the 'fold', he/she is OUT for the next round. The 'sheep' with the most 'food' at the end, wins!

2. Board Game

➤ In advance, design and make a simple board game. Have squares such as 'caught in thornbush - miss a turn', 'carried by shepherd - go forward two' etc. Perhaps also have forfeits (eg 'baa like a sheep')! Have a 'sheepfold' as the final square. ◄ Provide counters and dice. Have your youngsters play the game in small groups.

KEY VERSE: *[Jesus said:] "I am the Gate for the Sheep."* John 10:7

Checklist

☐ ....
☐ ....
☐ ....
☐ ....
☐ ....
☐ ....

Date ....

Planning Notes

Things to remember for next time...

TITLE: "I am the Real Vine..."

BIBLE BASE: John 15:1-17 (Jesus is Like a Vine)

WE WANT OUR YOUNGSTERS TO...

... understand that Jesus is asking us to follow Him closely;

... as appropriate, show love for Him and 'bear fruit' by really trying to keep His commandments.

LEAD-IN:

➤ In advance, draw and colour <u>or</u> make a collage of a tree trunk. Have branches cut out and ready to stick on - you will need one for every youngster. ◄ As your youngsters arrive, invite them to choose a branch, put their name on it, and stick it somewhere on the tree trunk.

HOW TO START:

◆ Using a mixture of questions and answers and short explanations, try to bring out the following points, as appropriate to the youngsters in your group:

- hold up a dead twig - ask: **will any leaves or fruit or berries ever grow on it? Why not?**
- unless the life of the tree flows into a twig, it cannot grow and bear fruit;
- Jesus said, *'I am the vine, and you are the branches'* (- a vine gives us grapes)...
- we will be filled with His life - His Spirit - if we stay joined to Him;
- ask: **how can we be joined to Jesus? How can we <u>stay</u> joined to Him?**
- when we follow Jesus and do what He asks us to, we are like a branch bearing beautiful fruit - this makes Jesus really happy!

◆ As appropriate, go back to the tree from the LEAD-IN. Write 'Jesus' on the trunk and add 'fruit' (ie 'being kind', 'helping other people meet Jesus' etc written on fruit shapes) - then pray.

ACTIVITIES:

1. 'Simon Says'

Give out simple instructions (eg jump up·and down, turn around etc). If your instructions begin with 'Simon says', the youngsters obey... if not, they don't! Anybody who obeys a false instruction is OUT for the next round. Point out that the key to doing well in the game was listening for 'Simon's' instructions and obeying them. Link this with the teaching content, as appropriate.

2. Tree Quiz

➤ In advance, prepare anagrams of some familiar fruit trees, (eg PLEAP, NANABA etc). Write each one on a separate piece of paper and number them. (Perhaps circle the first letter of each word, if your youngsters will need extra help to unravel them.) ◄ Stick them on the walls and furniture before your youngsters arrive. Ask your youngsters to get into pairs <u>or</u> three's. Give each pair a piece of paper and a pencil. Have the pairs go round the room and try to solve the anagrams! The pair with the most correct, wins.

KEY VERSE:

[Jesus said:] "I am the true vine, and you are the branches. If any remain in me and I remain in them, they produce much fruit." John 15:5

Checklist

☐ ....

☐ ....

☐ ....

☐ ....

☐ ....

☐ ....

Date ....

Planning Notes

Things to remember for next time...

TITLE: A Wedding

BIBLE BASE: John 2:1-12 (The Wedding at Cana)

WE WANT OUR YOUNGSTERS TO...

- ... know that Jesus went to special and happy events like weddings!
- ... be amazed at His power to change situations!
- ... celebrate!

LEAD-IN: Have everyone sitting down in a circle. Start with the sentence: "I went to a wedding and I gave the bride and groom... a toaster!" A youngster then continues: "I went to a wedding and I gave the bride and groom a toaster and a ....!", adding another suitable wedding present. Continue like this and see how long a list of wedding presents you can put together! If your youngsters will struggle to remember a list, just ask them to say the last four each time. Lead in by saying that when Jesus went to a wedding in Cana, he gave **everyone** a gift...

HOW TO START: ◆ Begin: *Everything was going so well! The wedding was wonderful: the bride and groom were very happy; the food was excellent; all the guests were having a great time... But then - disaster! The servants went to pour out some more wine, but it had all gone! Mary could see how upset and embarrassed the family was, so she went quietly to Jesus...*

ACTIVITIES: 1. Church Wedding

This is a brilliant opportunity to get your youngsters into a local church!
➤ In advance, arrange a brief visit with your minister. ◄ Ask him/her to just talk your youngsters through a wedding ceremony - you could maybe even get your youngsters to act one out! Talk sensitively but positively about God's ideas on marriage. Share stories of weddings you and your youngsters have been to...

2. Celebrate!

Talk together about other things we can celebrate (eg birthdays, the birth of a baby etc). As appropriate, say that all of these things are gifts from God... and He enjoys them too! Then celebrate in a way appropriate to your youngsters, eg
- Sing some praise songs;
- Play some party games;
- Make and share some simple food, such as:
  BANANA LOLLIES:
  Give each youngster half a peeled banana. Have everyone push a lolly stick carefully into the end. Help everyone dip the banana into clear honey <u>or</u> syrup, then roll it onto a plate of any coating you can provide (eg dessicated coconut, hundreds and thousands (chocolate or regular) etc).

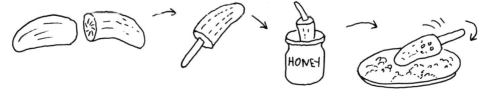

KEY VERSE: *Do whatever he tells you to do.* John 2:5

Checklist

☐ _____

☐ _____

☐ _____

☐ _____

☐ _____

☐ _____

Date _____

Planning Notes

Things to remember for next time...

TITLE: A Hungry Crowd

BIBLE BASE: John 6:1-15 (More than 5,000 Fed)

WE WANT OUR YOUNGSTERS TO...

    ... understand that something small can become something much greater in Jesus' hands!

    ... consider what they have to offer...

LEAD-IN: Provide simple food for a packed lunch (eg sliced bread, a couple of sandwich fillings, packets of crisps etc). Help each youngster make a sandwich and put together their own packed lunch <u>or</u> tea. Keep these to one side as you tell the story...

HOW TO START:
◆ Perhaps have someone tell the story from the boy's point of view: ***You'll never guess what happened to me today! I was just down by the boats when I heard a great crowd of people coming along the shore. They said that they were following a man called Jesus, so I thought I'd go with them! It was so brilliant being with Jesus! Nobody wanted to leave, but we were all starting to get hungry... Jesus' friends were worrying about where they could get enough food for us all. So I jumped up and offered them my lunch...!***

ACTIVITIES:

1. Packed Lunch

... Simply enjoy chatting together as your youngsters eat the packed lunches (<u>or</u> teas!) they made at the beginning of the session!

2. Share!

Talk together about sharing. Begin by asking for ideas of **what** your youngsters could share, (eg a toy, a meal, time, friendship, etc). Then talk about **how** they could share those things, (eg ask someone who often gets left out to join in a game, give a toy away etc). Bring out the idea that this small gift could be really 'big' for the person who receives it, (eg it doesn't 'cost' us much to include someone in a game... but it could make that person really happy!). As appropriate, ask your youngsters to decide on something they can share at some time after the session. Pray together, asking God to make these small gifts into something big!

KEY VERSE: *God loves the person who gives happily.* 2 Corinthians 9:7

Checklist

☐ ....
☐ ....
☐ ....
☐ ....
☐ ....
☐ ....

Date ....

Planning Notes

Things to remember for next time...

TITLE: A Sick Man

BIBLE BASE: Luke 5:12-16 (Jesus Heals a
Sick Man)

WE WANT OUR YOUNGSTERS TO...

> ... recognise how much Jesus cared
> for this man;
> ... see that He has the power to
> heal;
> ... be concerned for someone who is
> an outcast - and take appropriate
> action.

LEAD-IN: ➤ In advance, make up some 'odd one out' questions, (eg which is the odd
one out - orange, banana, bean, pineapple?). Choose things from your
youngsters' 'culture' (eg sport, music, TV etc). Have some picture clues too, if
possible. ◄ Either run this as a quiz in teams or do it altogether, just for fun
(eg a runaround quiz, with your youngsters running to the wall which
represents the 'odd one out' each time). Use this to help start a discussion
about how it feels to really be the 'odd one out'...

HOW TO START: ◆ ➤ In advance, think of words which describe the man both **before** and
after he met Jesus (ie ill, well, lonely, happy etc). For each one, write the
word and/or draw a simple picture to represent it on separate pieces of
paper - make them large enough for everyone to see. Do the same
with the words BEFORE and AFTER... ◄
◆ ... Tack BEFORE and AFTER side by side on a board or wall. Tack the other
words randomly underneath. As you tell the story, encourage your
youngsters to move these words to BEFORE or AFTER the man met Jesus.
◆ Begin: ***The man rubbed the skin on his arm, but the white patch would
not go away. His heart sank: he knew full well what the white patch
was...***

ACTIVITIES: **1. Outsiders Today...**

Remind your youngsters that the man was an 'outsider' before he met Jesus.
Talk together about the things which make.people 'outsiders' today. Now ask
your youngsters to get into pairs or small groups. Ask each group to either
work out a drama or draw a picture to show how an 'outsider' is treated by
others. Then ask them to act out or draw how Jesus would like the 'outsider'
to be treated. Have an opportunity to see each group's drama or picture.
Perhaps use this as a 'springboard' to talk about how your youngsters might
act towards the 'outsiders' they know of - then pray! [Be very sensitive! There
will be youngsters in your group who feel that they are 'outsiders'.]

2. Enjoy the Differences!

➤ In advance, think of about eight characteristics (eg hair, eyes, favourite
food, favourite sport etc). ◄ Ask everyone to run around. Shout out the first
characteristic: your youngsters must then get into a group in which everyone
is **different** (eg hair - short, long, curly, straight etc). The largest group each
time, wins the round. Do the same with the other characteristics. Use this to
talk about how good it is that we are all different - and challenge your
youngsters not to make someone an 'outsider' because he/she is different!

KEY VERSE: *[Jesus said:] "I tell you the truth, anything you did for even the least of my
people here, you also did for me."* Matthew 25:40

Checklist

☐ ....

☐ ....

☐ ....

☐ ....

☐ ....

☐ ....

Date ....

Planning Notes

Things to remember for next time...

TITLE: A Sick Girl

BIBLE BASE: Mark 5:21-43 (Jesus Gives Life to a Dead Girl and Heals a Sick Woman)

WE WANT OUR YOUNGSTERS TO...

... **be amazed that Jesus even has power over death!**
... **begin to trust that His power can change something in their lives which looks impossible.**

LEAD-IN: Teach some simple First Aid (eg show everybody how to bandage a cut <u>or</u> put an arm in a sling). Let the youngsters practise on each other! Talk together about how we care for people who are sick. If you know someone who works in health care, perhaps also invite him/her to talk about what he/she does.

HOW TO START: ◆ Begin: *Jairus was desperately worried. His little girl was terribly ill. The doctors said that they could do nothing to help. The little girl was going to die. Then someone told him about Jesus: "Jesus can heal people! You should take your daughter to see him. I'm sure that He will help!" Jairus knew that his daughter was far too ill to be moved from her bed, so he went to see Jesus himself...*

ACTIVITIES: ### 1. Newsflash!

<u>Either</u> in small groups <u>or</u> altogether, make a radio <u>or</u> TV report of the story. Have youngsters play different roles: reporters, Jairus and his daughter, people in the crowd. Interview them and talk about the issues (eg perhaps some people did not believe that the little girl really was brought back from the dead?) <u>Alternatively</u>, simply set up a drama to re-enact the events - ➤ you may want to write a simple script in advance for your youngsters to practise and perform. ◄

2. Prayer 'Bandage'

Ask your youngsters to tell you about people they know who are ill. Write their names on a strip of bandage <u>or</u> material for everyone to see as you go along. Talk about how they can be helped. Pray together for them. You could also tie a short strip of bandage <u>or</u> material around each youngster's wrist to remind him/her to continue to pray after this session. Remember to talk about these people from time to time - point out how God has answered prayer and that Jesus is just as powerful today! But be ready to help youngsters understand if someone has not got better...

KEY VERSE: *Jesus Christ is the same yesterday, today and for ever.* Hebrews 13:8

Checklist

- [ ] BANDAGES
- [ ] WHAT TO TAKE TO HOSPITAL
- [ ] DO YOU KNOW ANYONE WHO U [?]
- [ ] PRAYER
- [ ] MAKE GET WELL CARD
- [ ] THANK YOU FOR OUR HEALTH + PRAY FOR OTHERS
  READING

Planning Notes

Date ....

Things to remember for next time...

TITLE:	A Stormy Sea

BIBLE BASE: Matthew 8:23-27 (Jesus Calms a Storm)

WE WANT OUR YOUNGSTERS TO...

... **be amazed that Jesus has power over the forces of nature;**

... **begin to trust Him in situations which make them afraid.**

LEAD-IN: Play a version of 'Captain's Coming'! Have all your youngsters stand in the middle of your meeting room to begin with. Explain your 'orders': 'PORT!' = all run to left-hand wall; 'STARBOARD!' = all run to right; 'FORE!' = all run to front; 'AFT!' = all run to back; 'NETS OUT!' = mime throwing nets overboard; 'NETS FULL!' = mime pulling nets in; 'RAISE THE SAIL!' = mime pulling rope down. Call the orders out randomly! The last youngster to 'obey' each order is OUT: he/she decides who is last to obey the next order, swaps with him/her and is back in the game for the next round.

HOW TO START: ◆ Ask your youngsters to get into three groups:

Group A: works together to make a large boat from cardboard boxes, a broom handle, old cloth... any materials you can provide!

Group B: works together to produce sound effects - water, waves, wind, thunder, sea birds - using anything you can provide!

Group C: practises acting out the roles of Jesus and his disciples.

◆ Tell the story, including contributions from all the groups. If you have a large sheet <u>or</u> parachute, get your youngsters to sit all the way around it, take hold of the edge, and move it up and down to represent the sea - you can then have all the story action take place on and around it!

ACTIVITIES: **1. Thinking it Through...**

Ask your youngsters to get into small groups with a leader. Begin by asking: **what were Jesus' disciples afraid of?** Go on to ask about other things which are frightening (eg the dark). Talk together about what really frightens your youngsters... Explain simply how Jesus understands fears and is always with us when we are frightened. Finish by asking your youngsters to write <u>or</u> draw their fears on a small piece of paper, which they stick to the boat from the story. Then pray!

2. Key Verse

Give each youngster a piece of card (about the size of a post card). Ask everyone to draw on the card the things which frighten them. Then give them a thick, coloured pen. Have them write the KEY VERSE in bold letters right over the top of their fears! Talk together about the verse. Encourage your youngsters to carry the card with them and look at it whenever they are frightened!

KEY VERSE: *Don't be afraid, because I am with you.* Isaiah 43:5

Checklist

- [ ] BOXES
- [ ] SEA
- [ ] POSTERS - AFTER
      NOTES - SHIPS
      + FWIZ.
- [ ] GAME - NETS
      IN ETC
- [ ] AFRAID - WHAT
      OF? - JESUS
      ALWAYS THERE

Planning Notes

Date ....

Things to remember for next time...

TITLE: Saul's Conversion

BIBLE BASE: Acts 9:1-31 (Saul is Converted)

WE WANT OUR YOUNGSTERS TO...

... see that Jesus turned Saul's life around;

... know that He can do this for us too!

Paul
1 of 5

LEAD-IN: Draw each of the following road signs on separate pieces of paper, large enough for your youngsters to see.

  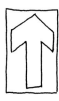 

RED   GREEN

Talk together about what each one means. Then ask your youngsters to run about in any direction, watching where they are going all the time! Hold up a road sign at a time - your youngsters have to obey it straightaway. The last person to do this after each sign change is OUT for the next round. Tack the signs up for everyone to see...

HOW TO START:

◆ Use the road signs as you tell the story. Stop several times and ask: **which sign goes with this bit of the story?** (eg STOP when Saul met Jesus; GIVE WAY to what Jesus wanted etc). <u>Alternatively</u>, use the signs to help your youngsters recall the main points of the story after you have told it.

◆ Begin: *"I hate those Christians!" growled Saul as he got ready to go to Damascus...*

◆ Interview another leader (<u>or</u> a guest) about how his/her life was changed after he/she met Jesus...

ACTIVITIES:

1. Personality Auction

➤ In advance, make a list of about ten characteristics you might find in a friend (eg generous, fun to be with, polite etc - make sure that there is a mixture of good and not-so-good!) ◄ Give £100 in Monopoly money (<u>or</u> make your own) to each youngster. Have an auction, letting your youngsters bid for any characteristic they would like in their best friend. Then talk together about which characteristics God changed in Saul - and which He might like to change in us!

2. Butterfly Mobile

Firstly, talk briefly about a caterpillar changing into a butterfly... and liken this to what happens when we become a Christian (see KEY VERSE). Then help your youngsters make a butterfly to hang from the ceiling to remind them of this. You could do this quite simply with paper and paints or pens (and a length of sewing cotton to hang each butterfly by). <u>Alternatively</u>, 'Fantasy Film' would be good (if you have a bit more money to spend!).

KEY VERSE: *If anyone belongs to Christ, there begins a new creation.* 2 Corinthians 5:17a

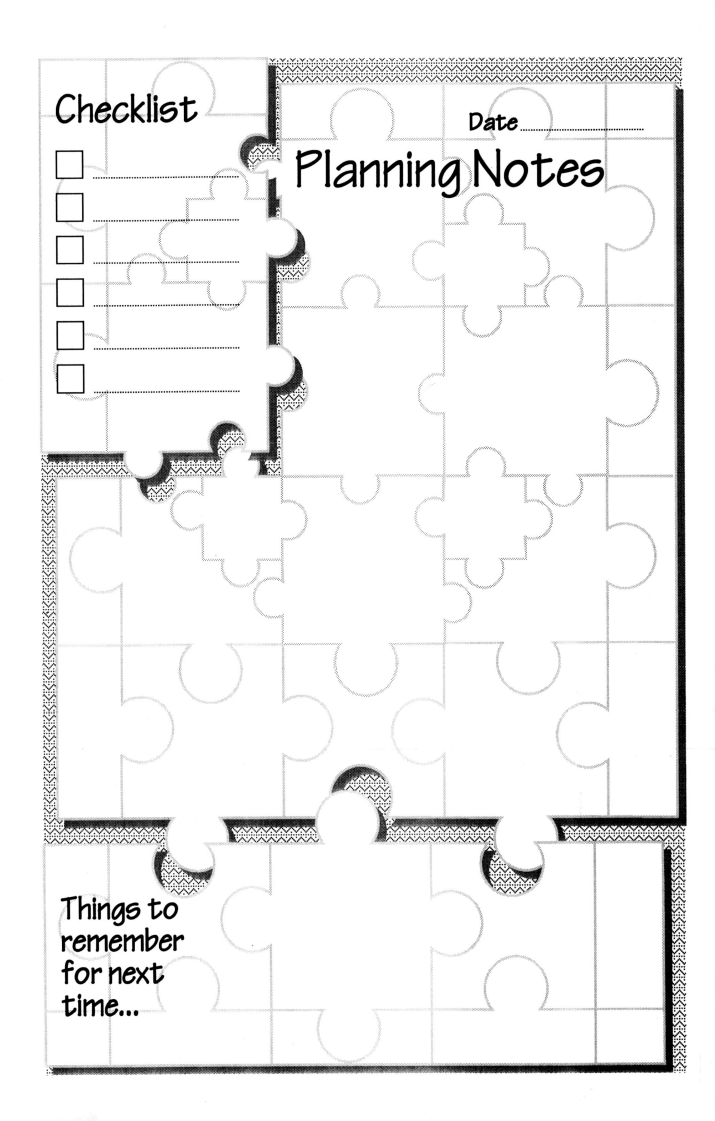

Checklist

☐ ....
☐ ....
☐ ....
☐ ....
☐ ....
☐ ....

Date ....

Planning Notes

Things to
remember
for next
time...

TITLE: Paul and Elymas

BIBLE BASE: Acts 13:1-12 (Barnabas and Saul in Cyprus)

WE WANT OUR YOUNGSTERS TO...

... think who they are most like in this story: those who listened and obeyed the Holy Spirit; Sergius Paulus, who was <u>trying</u> to listen; or Elymas, who not only refused to listen but also tried to prevent someone else from doing so!

LEAD-IN: Work out and practise a short and simple skit with another leader: you are trying to explain a game (<u>or</u> a joke <u>or</u> an important piece of information - make sure it's something your youngsters will really want to hear!), but the other leader keeps interrupting (eg by coming in late, asking stupid questions, falling off his/her chair etc). Ask: **what was it like not to be able to listen? Can you think of other times when someone or something stops you listening to something you want to hear?**

HOW TO START: ◆ Present this as a TV report, perhaps using audio cassette <u>or</u> video if you can.
◆ Begin by recapping what happened last session, then say something like: *'I'm now on the island of Cyprus, following Saul (now known as Paul). Saul - I mean Paul - has travelled here with Barnabas and John-Mark. Sergius Paulus, the governor of the island himself, has asked to speak with them. But this seems to have made Elymas very angry...'*

ACTIVITIES: **1. Follow-up Discussion**

➤ In advance, prepare a list of things which stop us listening to God - make sure they are relevant to your youngsters. Include a mixture of outside distractions ("my friend put me off") and personal attitudes ("I can't be bothered!"). ◄ Write your list on a large piece of paper, but cover up each individual statement with a strip of paper. Say what your list is about, then ask your youngsters to guess what is it... Uncover each distraction as your youngsters guess it. Then ask them to choose which three would be most likely to stop people of their age listening to God. <u>Either</u> altogether <u>or</u> in small groups, see if your youngsters can come up with creative (but practical) ideas to get round them. Then pray!

2. Zoom! Screech! Whoosh!

This is a standard 'Circle Game'. The leader picks someone in the circle to begin. This player turns and says 'zoom' to the person on their left who can then:
• say 'zoom' to continue the play round the circle;
• say 'screech' to change the direction of play;
• say 'whoosh' <u>and</u> point to pass the play to someone else in the circle.
When someone makes a mistake, he/she is OUT <u>or</u> does a forfeit. Point out that the key to doing well was listening carefully and not being distracted. Link this with the teaching content, as appropriate.

KEY VERSE: *Come to me and listen; listen to me that you may live.* Isaiah 55:3

Checklist

☐ ....

☐ ....

☐ ....

☐ ....

☐ ....

☐ ....

Date ....

Planning Notes

Things to remember for next time...

TITLE: Paul and a Prison Officer

BIBLE BASE: Acts 16:16-40 (Paul and Silas in Jail)

WE WANT OUR YOUNGSTERS TO...
- ... see that people in the world have power and authority, but God is really in charge!
- ... trust God in hard times.

LEAD-IN: Choose two youngsters: one is the 'jailer' and the other the 'prisoner'. Ask the rest of the group to hold hands and form a circle - the 'prison walls'! Put the 'prisoner' inside the circle and have the 'jailer' patrol round the outside. The 'prisoner' can escape by leaving the circle at any time. As soon as he/she has left the circle, the 'jailer' has a count of 12 to recapture him/her: both youngsters can run in and out of the circle by going over or under the linked hands. Repeat several times, with different youngsters taking turns.

HOW TO START:
- ◆ Carry on the reporter theme, perhaps interviewing the slave girl and then the prison officer...
- ◆ Begin: *'I've followed Paul to the city of Philippi and am now standing outside the prison. Paul and his new companion, Silas, are being held prisoner here. But they haven't committed a crime...'*
- ◆ Ask: **how come Paul and Silas were singing happy songs in jail?!** Clearly and simply bring out their joy in God, whatever was happening to them. Help your youngsters think about this for their own lives - then pray!

ACTIVITIES: **1. Drama**

Ask your youngsters to get into groups of about four. Divide the story into separate parts (eg the healing of the slave girl; Paul and Silas in court etc) and ask each group to prepare and act out one of the scenes. Try and have each group's performance follow straight on from the previous one, so that everyone gets a feel for the whole story.

2. Quiz

➤ In advance, make up about 12 questions on this event. Also, make two paper chains, each with six large links in. ◀ Organise your youngsters into two teams. Have one youngster from each team 'imprisoned' with paper chains. Ask the questions to each team in turn - each correct answer breaks one of the paper links. At the end, remind your youngsters about who really broke the chains for Paul and Silas...!

KEY VERSE: *Come, let us sing for joy to the Lord.* Psalm 95:1

Checklist

- ☐ ....
- ☐ ....
- ☐ ....
- ☐ ....
- ☐ ....
- ☐ ....

Date ....

Planning Notes

Things to remember for next time...

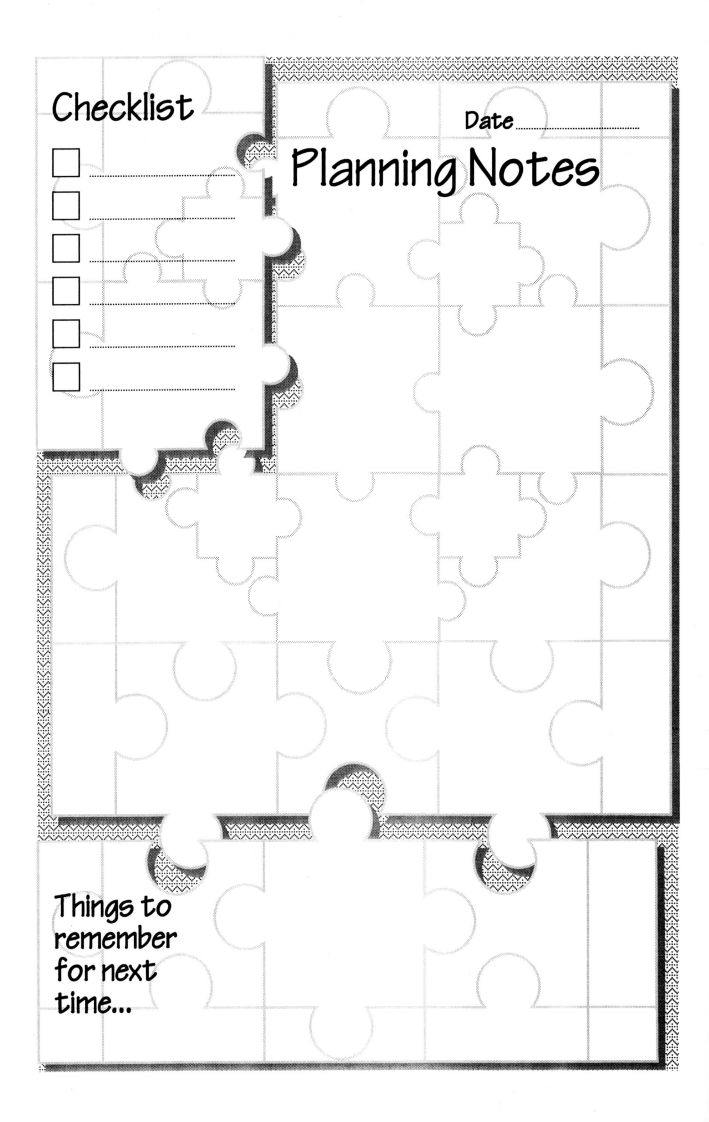

TITLE: Paul and a Silversmith

BIBLE BASE: **Acts 19:21-41** (Trouble in Ephesus)

WE WANT OUR YOUNGSTERS TO...
... hear that there is only one GOD!
... know that we cannot control God.

LEAD-IN: ➤ In advance, get together some things which are 'original' with their imitations (eg butter & margarine, Coca-cola & a supermarket brand, silk & polyester etc). ◄ Have your youngsters look, taste and feel (as appropriate!) and then take a vote on which is the real thing each time - was anyone fooled by the imitations?

HOW TO START: ◆ Carry on the reporter theme...
◆ Begin: *'Amazing scenes here in Ephesus! I'm standing outside the magnificent temple of the goddess Artemis. Demetrius, a local silversmith, has got rich by making models of Artemis and selling them to people who visit the temple. But now Paul and the other followers of Jesus are saying   that there is only one God and that Artemis is just a fake...!'*

ACTIVITIES: **1. T-Shirts**

➤ In advance, cut simple T-shirt shapes out of paper. ◄ Give one to each youngster. Ask everyone to design a T-shirt which points to the One True God. Have an opportunity to enjoy everyone's ideas.

2. Model-making

Have your youngsters make models with any materials you have available (eg wood, clay, Fimo etc). Take the opportunity to point out how silly it would be to treat one of these models as if it were God!! As appropriate, talk simply and clearly about the things we do turn into gods.

KEY VERSE: *You are great and you do miracles. Only you are God.* Psalm 86:10

Checklist

- [ ] ....
- [ ] ....
- [ ] ....
- [ ] ....
- [ ] ....
- [ ] ....

Date ....

Planning Notes

Things to remember for next time...

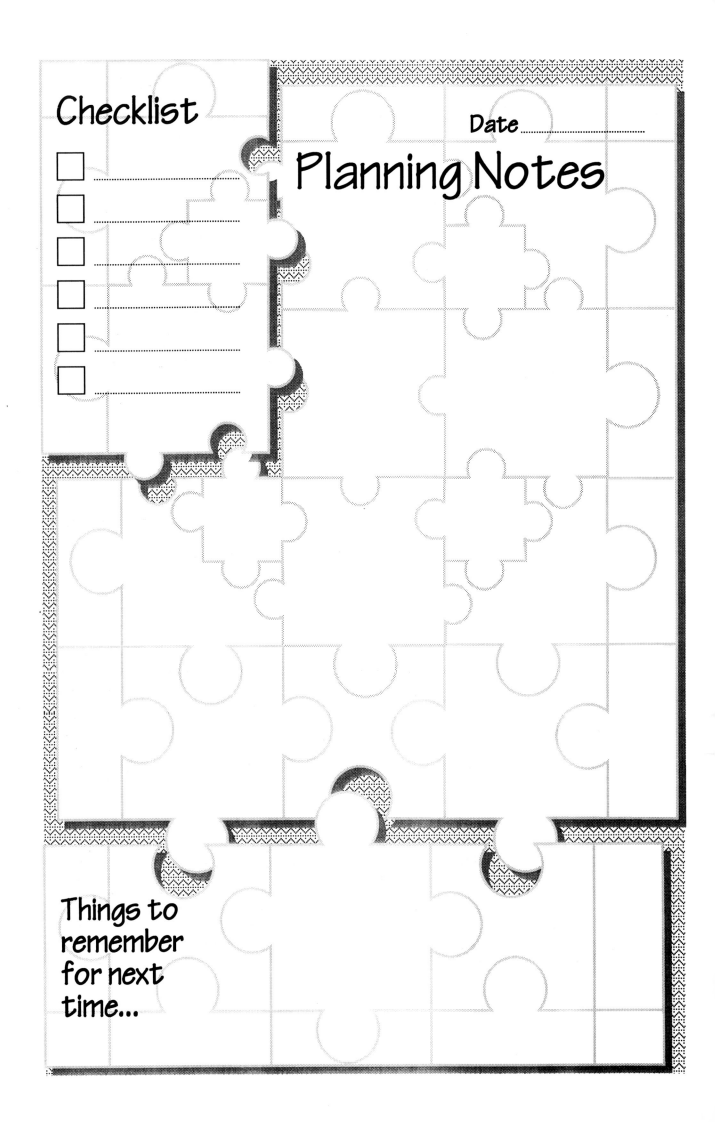

TITLE: Paul Shipwrecked

BIBLE BASE: **Acts 27:1-44** (*from* Paul Sails for Rome *to* The Ship is Destroyed)

WE WANT OUR YOUNGSTERS TO...

... **know that God is with us in danger;**

... **see that Paul knew what to do because God told him... and God always knows best!**

LEAD-IN: Talk sensitively together about being in danger. Maybe tell your youngsters about a time when you were in danger - and bring out clearly how God helped you through the situation. Go on to ask your youngsters about similar experiences they have had and about how it feels to be in danger...

HOW TO START:
- ➤ In advance, choose six key words form the story (eg sailors, sea, Paul, prisoners etc). ◄
- Have your youngsters get into teams of about six. Give each team member one of the key words (ie the first person in each team is always 'prisoner' and so on.) Then read the story in *Acts 27:20-44* from a suitable Bible translation... Whenever someone hears the word he/she was given, he/she runs to the end of the hall and back - the first one to do this scores a point for his/her team each time.
- ...With all this activity, your youngsters may have missed a few points, so ask some questions at the end to fill in the details!

ACTIVITIES:

1. Shipwreck A

➤ In advance, collect together <u>two</u> of each of a whole range of things you might have on a journey (eg large bags, teddy bears, books, coats etc) - the more, the better! ◄ Have your youngsters get into two teams. Position each team in a 'ship' at one end of your meeting room and 'load' everything 'on board'. Also, give each team two large mats (<u>or</u> sheets of newspaper). When you shout 'shipwreck!', each team must get to 'dry land' (ie the other end of your meeting room) without going in the 'sea' (ie touching the floor)... the way to do this is to keep throwing out the mats for everyone and (everything!) to move onto, so be ready to suggest this if your youngsters need help!

2. Shipwreck B

➤ In advance, work out some actions to go with things you might do on a ship (eg holding your tummy = feeling unwell! etc) ◄ Make a 'ship' with a circle of chairs (<u>or</u> similar) at one end of your meeting room and have everyone get 'on board'. Explain the actions. Call them out randomly... When you shout 'shipwreck!', everyone has to 'swim' (ie run) to 'dry land' (ie the other end of your meeting room) - you could vary this too (eg by saying that the 11 year olds should 'rescue' a younger child etc). If you wish, give a small sweet to the first youngsters to reach 'dry land' each time.

KEY VERSE: *[God] knows everything.* 1 John 3:20

Checklist

☐ ....

☐ ....

☐ ....

☐ ....

☐ ....

☐ ....

Date ....

Planning Notes

Things to remember for next time...

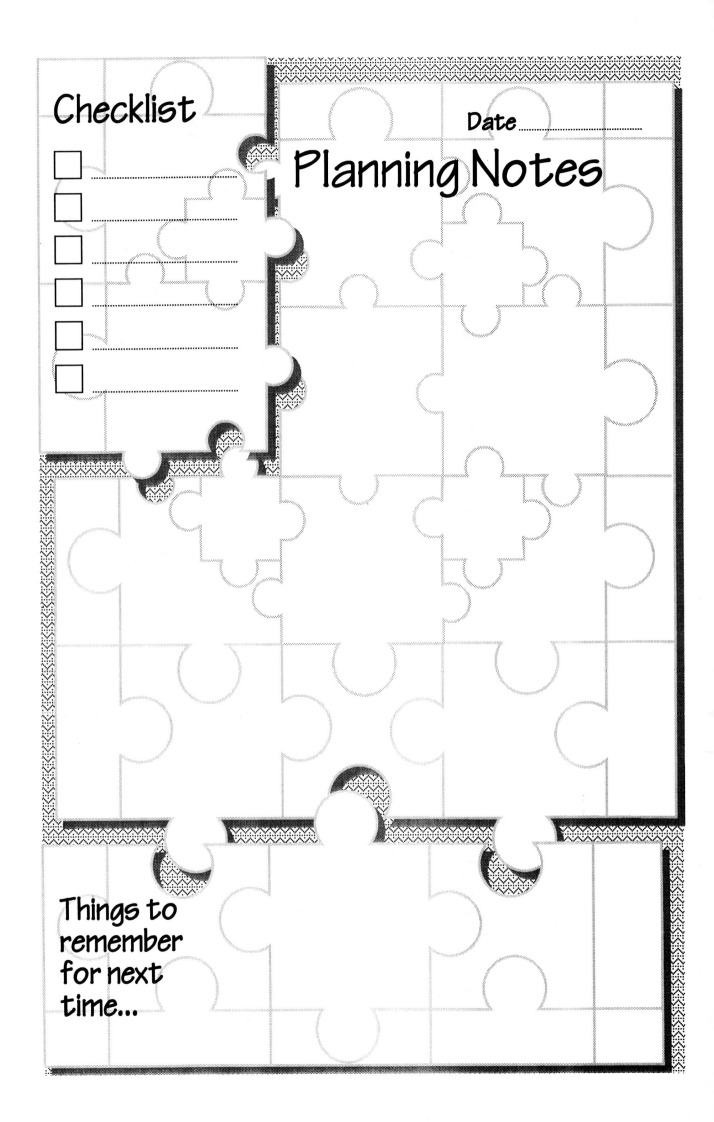

TITLE: ...Praising

BIBLE BASE: Nehemiah 1:1-5 (Nehemiah's Prayer)

WE WANT OUR YOUNGSTERS TO...

... appreciate that God deserves - and enjoys! - our love and praise;

... understand that prayer should include these things;

... pray!

LEAD-IN: ➤ In advance, collect a few pictures of current 'heroes' (eg singers, sports personalities etc). ◄ Just talk generally about them. Ask your youngsters to say what is good about each one - perhaps note these things down as you go along. Talk together about how much we enjoy what these people do and about how we show our appreciation.

HOW TO START: ◆ ➤ As you tell Nehemiah's story over the next four sessions, it would be good to have a visual presentation appropriate to the age group you're working with, so prepare something in advance! You could have simple puppets (which your youngsters could make and/or 'work') or a simple picture board (with cut-out figures to make and/or move) or a series of OHP slides... ◄

◆ Introduce Nehemiah: his life in exile, his job tasting wine, his love of God etc.

◆ Begin: ***Nehemiah worked for King Artaxerxes, the most important man in the whole empire! Although he respected the king, Nehemiah saved his praise and admiration for someone else...***

◆ Highlight the fact that Nehemiah began his prayer by praising God!

ACTIVITIES:

1. Praise God!

Aim to help your youngsters praise God - or at least take steps towards this! It may be appropriate to just help them become more aware of what God is like: linking in with the LEAD-IN, perhaps write and/or draw some characteristics of God (eg love, power etc) on separate pieces of paper and ask your youngsters to choose which one they like best! Perhaps.then ask your youngsters to get into a line and take one step forward every time they think of something to praise God for. You could then lead on to simple, one sentence prayers of praise to God (eg 'I like it that you are kind' etc) and/or have some worship songs. Make sure that your youngsters can really be a part of whatever you choose... otherwise it will be a performance from you and mean nothing to anyone else!

2. Jerusalem Model

Have your youngsters make a simple model replica of Jerusalem and the walls, using whatever materials you can provide! You could begin the model this week and carry on building over the next **two** sessions!

KEY VERSE: *Through Jesus let us always offer to God our sacrifice of praise.* Hebrews 13:15

Checklist

☐ _____

☐ _____

☐ _____

☐ _____

☐ _____

☐ _____

Date _____

Planning Notes

Things to remember for next time...

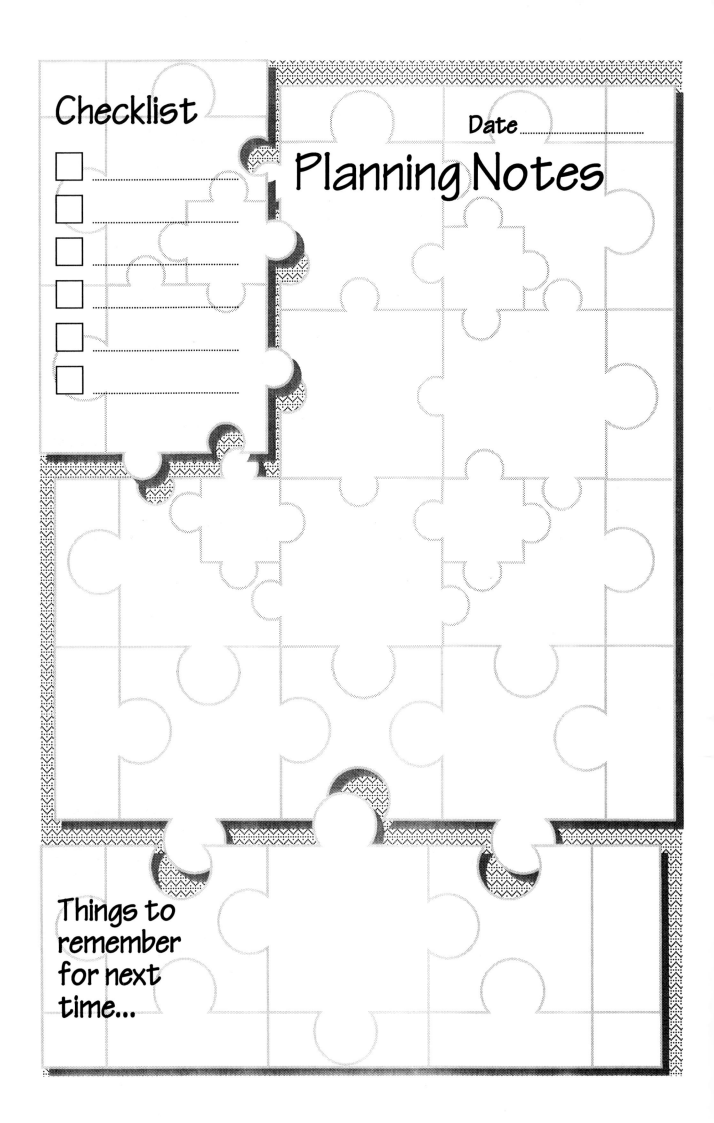

TITLE: ...Saying 'Sorry'

BIBLE BASE: **Nehemiah 1:2-7** (Nehemiah's Prayer)

WE WANT OUR YOUNGSTERS TO...

... **understand why we need to be honest with God about the things we have done wrong and be forgiven by Him;**

... **pray!**

LEAD-IN:

➤ In advance, think of a situation relevant to your youngsters in which someone does something wrong (eg breaking a window). Work out a short drama about it - include a positive ending when the person 'owns up'! ◄ Act out the drama, but stop just after the incident! Then ask: **should he/she 'own up'? What would happen if he/she did? What would happen if he/she did not?** Help your youngsters talk about similar incidents from their own lives (ie **why is it hard to 'own up'?**) Show the rest of the drama: highlight the good that came out of 'owning up', but be aware that your youngsters may have had much less positive experiences of doing this... State briefly but clearly that 'owning up' to God is <u>always</u> a good thing and <u>never</u> gets us punished...

HOW TO START:

◆ Remind your youngsters about Nehemiah's situation.
◆ Explain briefly that Nehemiah did not try to blame everyone else for what had happened - he knew that he needed to 'own up' to God about the wrong things he and his people had done...
◆ ...he also knew that God would forgive and forget - completely! (As appropriate, link in with the LEAD-IN.)
◆ Read Nehemiah's prayer from the Bible <u>or</u> put it into your own words.
◆ In a very short time of quiet, invite your youngsters to simply 'own up' to God about anything they know they have done wrong. Finish with a spoken prayer yourself - and remind your youngsters that they might need to say 'sorry' to someone else as well.

ACTIVITIES:

1. Jerusalem Model

...Continue building your replica of Jerusalem!

2. Key Verse

In advance, write out the KEY VERSE using something that can be easily wiped away, (eg chalk, dry-wipe pens on a white board etc). Read it through together. Explain that 'confess' is another way of saying 'own up'. Then help your youngsters learn it by having them wipe away a few words at a time - if you begin with 'sins' and 'wrongs', you can use this to reinforce the teaching points!

KEY VERSE:

If we confess our sins (...) He will make us clean from all the wrongs we have done. 1 John 1:9

Checklist

- ☐ ....
- ☐ ....
- ☐ ....
- ☐ ....
- ☐ ....
- ☐ ....

Date ....

Planning Notes

Things to remember for next time...

TITLE: ...Asking

BIBLE BASE: **Nehemiah 1:10-2:18**
(Nehemiah is Sent to Jerusalem
& Nehemiah Inspects Jerusalem)

WE WANT OUR YOUNGSTERS TO...

    ... **know that God invites us to talk
to Him about everything we need;**

    ... **pray - for others and for
themselves.**

LEAD-IN: Have a 'Team Building Challenge'! Ask your
youngsters to get into small teams of about six. Give
each group the same number of 'building blocks' - these could be playing
cards or newspapers or paper cups or empty cartons or marshmallows...
whatever you have available! Now set the teams the challenge of building the
tallest or strongest wall. Stop after about five minutes and judge each team's
efforts! Then talk together about what you would really need to build a wall...

HOW TO START: ◆ Begin: *Nehemiah desperately wanted to re-build the walls of Jerusalem -
but how could he? He was hundreds of miles away from Jerusalem and
he could not just go there whenever he wanted. And besides, where
would he get the building materials? And the tools? And the people to
do the job? Nehemiah asked God for what he needed, and then he
waited...*

    ◆ Bring out clearly that God really enjoys it when we spend time asking Him
for what we need - and for what other people need too!

ACTIVITIES: **1. Jerusalem Model & Prayer Wall**

...Finish building your replica of Jerusalem! Then have your youngsters write
or draw on small pieces of paper anything they would like to ask God for.
Have these tacked onto the wall you have built, near the base if possible. Pray
about these things altogether or in small groups or individually. Keep your
'Prayer Wall' on display over the next few months. Keep up-to-date on the
situations, perhaps moving the pieces of paper up the wall when the requests
are answered. Be ready to help your youngsters deal with any requests which
are not answered as they might have hoped...

2. 'Outburst'!

➤ In advance, think of about ten things Nehemiah needed to build the walls of
Jerusalem... including prayer! Write or draw these things on separate pieces
of paper - you will need one set of these 'building cards' for every six
youngsters, so repeat as necessary. ◀ Ask your youngsters to get into teams
of six with one leader per team. Station the leaders at one end of your
meeting room and the teams at the other! Give each leader a set of the
'building cards'. On the word 'go', one person from each team runs to their
leader and says **one** thing they think Nehemiah needed to build the walls: if
this is on one of the 'building cards', the leader gives the youngster the card...
if not, he/she runs straight back to his/her team. The first team to collect all
the cards in this way, wins!

KEY VERSE: *Do not worry about anything, but pray and ask God for everything you need,
always giving thanks.* Philippians 4:6

Checklist

- ☐ ....
- ☐ ....
- ☐ ....
- ☐ ....
- ☐ ....
- ☐ ....

Date ....

Planning Notes

Things to remember for next time...

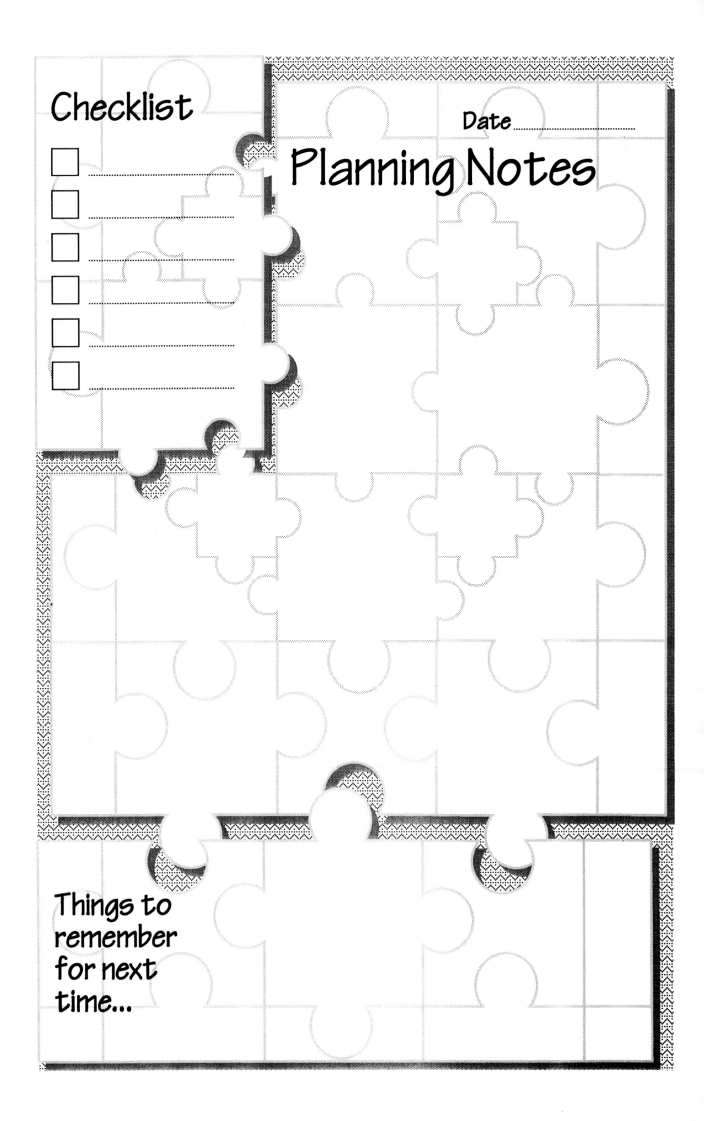

TITLE: ...Giving Thanks

BIBLE BASE: Nehemiah 9:6-25 (The People's Prayer)

WE WANT OUR YOUNGSTERS TO...

... be aware of all we have thank God for;

... pray!

LEAD-IN:

➤ In advance, make up a short play in which someone gives something to someone else... and that person just takes it without thanks. ◄ Have leaders <u>and/or</u> youngsters act it out in front of everybody. Talk together about how the 'giver' might feel... and then about any similar experiences you and your youngsters have had.

HOW TO START:

◆ Tell the story of the walls being rebuilt (skipping over much of the detail found in the Bible, of course!);

◆ Begin: **Nehemiah could hardly believe his eyes and ears! Everywhere he looked there were people moving stones and timber, hammering and chopping... It was amazing...!**

◆ End by telling how the people thanked God for all that He had done for them;

◆ If appropriate, challenge your youngsters about what they do when God does something for them... do they go back and say 'thank you' to Him? Perhaps link this with your PRAYER WALL from last session.

ACTIVITIES:

1. Thank You Card

Ask your youngsters to think of someone who often does things for them and whom they perhaps take for granted... Have them design, colour and decorate a simple card (using any materials you can provide) to say 'thank you' to that person. <u>Alternatively</u>, have the group make a large 'thank you' card and write <u>or</u> draw inside things to be thankful to God for!

2. Thank You, Lord...

➤ In advance, think of a <u>**wide**</u> range of things God gives us (eg friends, food, healthy bodies, the world, Jesus, His love, His forgiveness etc). Write <u>and/or</u> draw <u>and/or</u> stick a picture of each thing on a separate piece of paper. Do as many of these as you can to highlight the fact that God gives us so much! Hide them all around your meeting room before the session. ◄ Ask your youngsters to get into groups of about six. Send them to find as many of the hidden pieces of paper as they can and bring them back to their group. Have each group spread out all their pieces of paper. Then help your youngsters use them as a basis for their own prayers.

KEY VERSE:

Pray continually, and give thanks whatever happens. This is what God wants for you in Christ Jesus. 1 Thessalonians 5:18

Checklist

☐ ....

☐ ....

☐ ....

☐ ....

☐ ....

☐ ....

Date ....

Planning Notes

Things to
remember
for next
time...

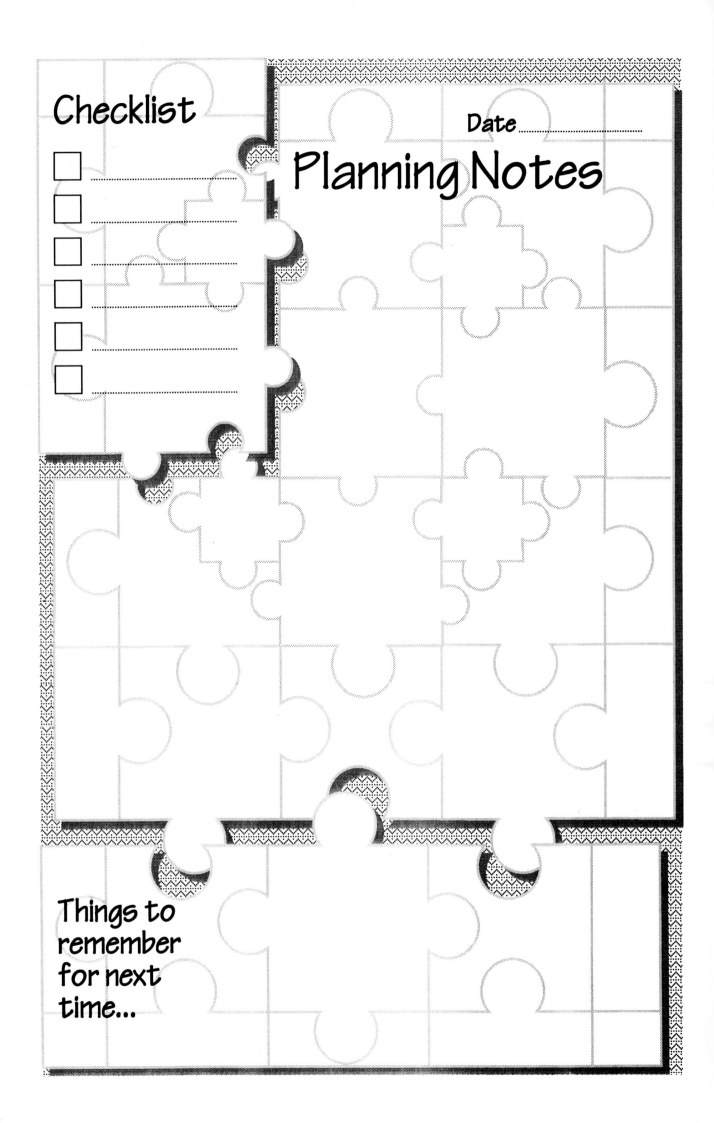

TITLE: The Door

BIBLE BASE: Revelation 3:14-22 (To the Church in Laodicea)

WE WANT OUR YOUNGSTERS TO...

... understand that Jesus wants to be involved in all of our lives;
... know that it's not good enough to be lukewarm about God.

LEAD-IN: Share some 'knock, knock' jokes – but make sure you set clear guidelines at the outset about what is and isn't acceptable in a joke!

HOW TO START:
◆ ➤ In advance, make a 'letter', which is a very simple version of the message to the church in Laodicea. You could write it by hand <u>or</u> make it look like an e-mail. ◄
◆ Begin: *Soon after Jesus went back to Heaven, John was sent away to a remote island - just because he was a Christian! One Sunday, John was praying when he heard a loud voice behind him – it was Jesus!! Jesus gave John some urgent messages to write down and send...*
◆ Have your youngsters read the 'letter', explaining that it contains one of the messages Jesus gave John.
◆ Focus on the facts that:
 • <u>Jesus said that the church was lukewarm</u>. Ask your youngsters what they think this means. Explain that the people at the church could not decide whether they wanted God in their lives or not.
 • <u>Jesus said that He is knocking at the door</u>. Get your youngsters to think about how they behave if a visitor comes to their house (eg If someone rings your doorbell, how long do they wait on the doorstep while you decide to let them in? Which rooms in the house are they allowed to go in? What would you eat and drink? What would you talk about? Would you share your secrets? etc). Explain that we can choose to let Jesus into our lives, or we can leave Him standing outside.

(**Extra:** Holman Hunt's picture 'Jesus, the Light of the World' could help here. Most Christian book shops will have a small copy with an explanation.)

ACTIVITIES:

1. Hot or Cold

➤ In advance, think of a list of foods – include some which can be eaten hot or cold. ◄ Have your youngsters stand in the middle of the room. Say that one wall is 'hot' and the other 'cold'. Call out each food in turn. Ask your youngsters to run to the wall which is the temperature they would like to eat the food at. Point out that no-one stayed in the middle (ie lukewarm) - and link with the teaching content.

2. Open the Door

Have your youngsters make a paper door and door frame. Help them write the first part of the KEY VERSE (ie up to 'open the door') on the outside, and the second part inside. (This could be done as a small, take-home individual item, <u>or</u> as a large, group work of art for your meeting room).

KEY VERSE: *[Jesus said:] "Here I am! I stand at the door and knock. If you hear my voice and open the door, I will come in and eat with you, and you will eat with me."*
Revelation 3:20

Checklist

☐ ....
☐ ....
☐ ....
☐ ....
☐ ....
☐ ....

Date ....

Planning Notes

Things to remember for next time...

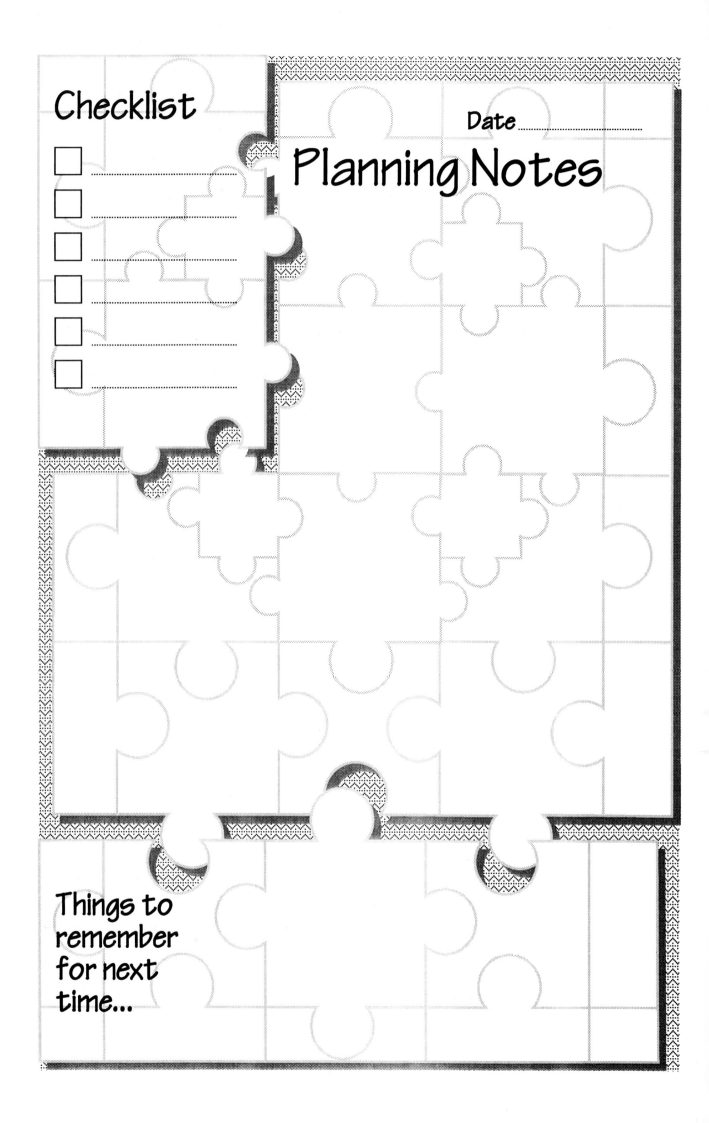

TITLE: The Crowd

BIBLE BASE: Revelation 4:1-6a (John Sees Heaven) & 7:9-17 (The Great Crowd Worships God)

WE WANT OUR YOUNGSTERS TO...

... be sure that Jesus is alive and reigns in Heaven now;

... hear that Heaven will be fun;

... know that there will be people of all races and backgrounds in Heaven.

LEAD-IN: Ask your youngsters: **have you ever been in a crowd... maybe at a football match, carnival or firework display?** Then have them talk about the experience. Be prepared to acknowledge that some of your youngsters may have had negative experiences of being in a crowd, but focus on positive memories and feelings. (If you have a large number of youngsters, perhaps try a 'Mexican Wave'!)

HOW TO START:

◆ Set the scene by showing a video clip of one of the 'Back to the Future' films (or similar!). Explain that one of the books in the Bible is a bit like that... and actually show them Revelation in a Bible.

◆ Begin: *This is the book of messages Jesus asked John to write down! Most of it is about the future. Jesus showed John all sorts of exciting things which are going to happen...*

◆ Perhaps ask your youngsters to close their eyes and imagine the scene as you describe it...

◆ Make sure you bring out clearly that:
  • <u>People will be in Heaven because they belong to Jesus</u> (- link with last session);
  • <u>There will be a huge crowd</u> of them!
  • <u>People from all over the world</u> will be in Heaven;
  • <u>Everyone will have a great time</u> praising God!

ACTIVITIES:

1. Picture the Crowd

Make a large 3-D collage of the crowd in Heaven. Make sure that it includes people from a wide variety of ethnic backgrounds. Scrunch up small balls of newspaper for peoples' heads and paint them in a variety of skin-colours. Add wool for hair and use scrap material to make clothes.

2. Hallelujah!

Teach this word to your youngsters and explain what it means! Ask them to get into small groups. Ask each small group to work out a short song <u>or</u> chant (with clapping etc) to praise God, using just the word 'hallelujah'. Have an opportunity to hear each group's ideas. Then combine them all, so that the whole group is singing and/or shouting at the same time! ➤ <u>Alternatively</u>, make up some songs, chants and rounds in advance for your whole group to do together, ◀ <u>or</u> teach some existing ones.

KEY VERSE: *You are worthy, our Lord and God, to receive glory and honour and power, because you made all things.* Revelation 4:11a

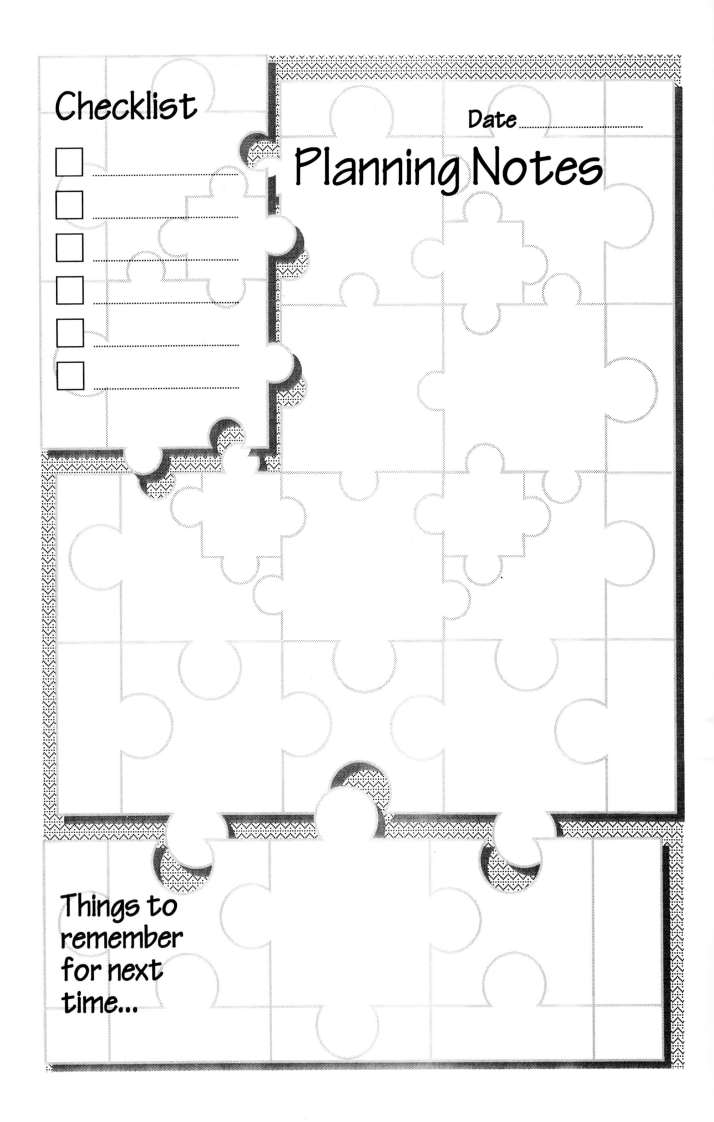

Checklist

☐ ....
☐ ....
☐ ....
☐ ....
☐ ....
☐ ....

Date ....

Planning Notes

Things to
remember
for next
time...

TITLE: The City

BIBLE BASE: Revelation 21:1-5 & 10-27
(The New Jerusalem)

WE WANT OUR YOUNGSTERS TO...

... **understand that Heaven is an
awesome place and that it's
absolutely perfect;**
... **want to go to Heaven.**

LEAD-IN: Talk together about all the things that are wrong
with wherever you live. Ask: **if you could design
the perfect city, what would it be like?** Provide some
pictures <u>and/or</u> video clips of different styles of architecture for inspiration – if
possible, have a mixture of old and new, real (eg New York) and science fiction
(eg Gotham City). Help your youngsters consider deeper issues than just the
appearance of the buildings.

HOW TO START:
◆ ➤ In advance, imagine that you are a tour guide and prepare to give your
group a 'conducted tour' of the heavenly city, which John saw. ◀ Also, if
you can, find pictures <u>or</u> real pieces(!) of some of the precious and semi-
precious stones mentioned.
◆ Give the 'conducted tour': focus on the facts that:
• <u>There are no tears or sadness in Heaven;</u>
• <u>Heaven is a really perfect place.</u>
◆ If your youngsters are keen on art, do not spend too long on this section,
but allow plenty of time for ACTIVITY 1 below: whilst you are doing this you
can explore the city further through discussions and answering questions.

ACTIVITIES: **1. Designer City**

➤ In advance, prepare a quantity of colourful art materials. You will need
background paper (wallpaper is good), large quantities of PVA glue, anything
which looks like precious stones (eg sweets, beads, sequins, or chopped-up
wax crayons) and any of the following: scraps of brightly coloured paper, card
or packaging; polystyrene foam; small cardboard boxes; aluminium foil; sweet
wrappers; small pebbles; pasta; lentils; sea shells; gold and/or silver spray
paint; cotton wool; wrapping paper; shiny fabric etc. ◀ Altogether <u>or</u> in small
groups, produce a magnificent collage of the heavenly city. Allow your
youngsters to use their imaginations, but encourage them to be as accurate to
the Bible text as possible. It may be helpful to have a Bible open at *Revelation
21* (wrapped in a clear plastic bag so that it can be referred to without the
pages being glued together!).

2. My Perfect Day

Continue the theme of 'perfection' by asking each person to describe his/her
perfect day - if appropriate, use the song 'Perfect Day' to get everyone
thinking... You could do this as an interview: why not make a recording of it
(on audio cassette <u>or</u> video) and play it back in a year's time?

KEY VERSE: *The One who was sitting on the throne said, "Look! I am making everything
new!"* Revelation 21:5

Checklist

- [ ] ....
- [ ] ....
- [ ] ....
- [ ] ....
- [ ] ....
- [ ] ....

Date ....

Planning Notes

Things to remember for next time...

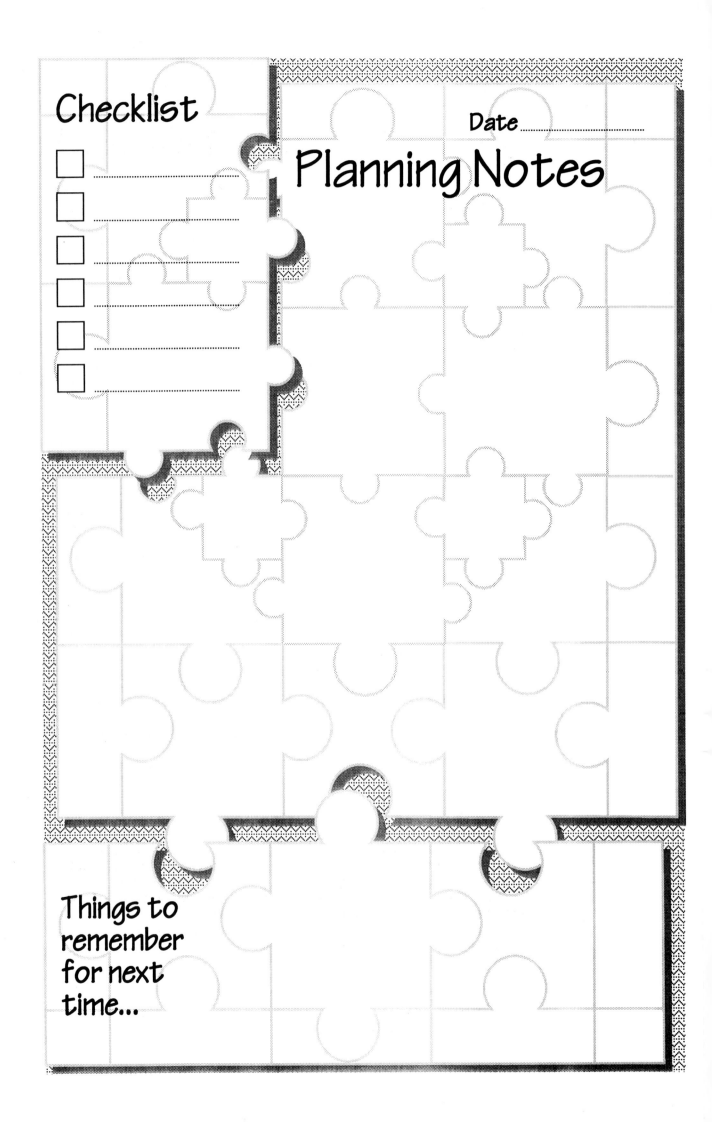

TITLE: The River and the Tree of Life

The End

BIBLE BASE: **Revelation 22:1-5** (The New Jerusalem) **& Genesis 2:9**

WE WANT OUR YOUNGSTERS TO...

... **understand that God heals, brings peace and gives life;**

... **know that there will be no more illness, sadness, war or death in Heaven.**

LEAD-IN: Ask your youngsters to get into teams of about four. Give each team a pen and paper. Give your youngsters 30 seconds to think of as many things as they can in the following three categories: types of tree; fruit which grows on trees; names of rivers. See which team has thought of the most things in each category and award prizes, as appropriate!

HOW TO START:
◆ ➤ In advance, find a picture of a tree and one of a river, large enough for everyone to see. ◀
◆ Remind your youngsters about the heavenly city from last session, using the collage they made.
◆ Talk about what is in the main street of your city or town... then describe the river and trees in the main street of the heavenly city. Focus on the facts that:
  • The fruit on the tree gives life – so the people in Heaven will live forever.
  • The leaves on the tree heal the nations – try to get your youngsters to think about what the nations need to be healed from (eg war, famine etc).
  • (This tree is mentioned right at the beginning of the Bible: in the book of Genesis, Adam and Eve were allowed to eat from the tree of life, before sin spoiled everything.)

ACTIVITIES: **1. The Tree of Life**

Make a 3D model of the tree of life, with fruit, flowers and leaves. 'Dip-it Fantasy Film' (available from specialist art suppliers) would be really good - but it is expensive! You could also use wire and mod-roc (and paint it afterwards), or pipe-cleaners and tissue paper.

2. Prayer Tree

➤ In advance, cut out a tree trunk shape from brown paper and stick it to a larger piece of backing paper. Also, cut out lots of large leaves from light green paper. ◀ Ask your youngsters to think of: 1) people who are sick; 2) places in the world where there are wars, famines or other disasters. Write each person and place on a separate 'leaf' and tack them on the 'tree'. Pray, either aloud or in silence, asking God to bring about healing. If you wish, continue to refer to the 'prayer tree' over the next few sessions, adding 'leaves' as appropriate.

KEY VERSE: *God will wipe away every tear from their eyes, and there will be no more death, sadness, crying or pain, because all the old ways are gone.*

Revelation 21:4

Checklist

- ☐ ....
- ☐ ....
- ☐ ....
- ☐ ....
- ☐ ....
- ☐ ....

Date ....

Planning Notes

Things to remember for next time...

TITLE: The Wedding Feast

BIBLE BASE: Matthew 25:1-13 (A Story
About Ten Bridesmaids);
Revelation 19:7-8 & 21:2

WE WANT OUR YOUNGSTERS TO...

... hear that Jesus is coming back
again - which is something to
celebrate;

... be ready for Jesus' return.

LEAD-IN: Talk together about weddings your youngsters have
been to. ➤ Perhaps ask someone in advance to bring in
something from a wedding (eg clothes, photos, invitations etc). ◄ Ask if
anyone has been a bridesmaid or page boy. Compare different wedding
customs. Talk in particular about what a bridesmaid has to do.

HOW TO START: ◆ Begin: *The bride was ready, the ten bridesmaids were ready... they were*
all in the bride's house, waiting for the groom. It was so exciting! Each
bridesmaid had an oil lamp, ready for the wedding procession through
the dark streets. The groom would arrive any minute... wouldn't he...?
◆ Explain that:
  • Jesus told this story.
  • <u>Jesus is like the bridegroom</u>, because one day he is coming back to earth
    again – then there will be the most fantastic party (like the best ever
    wedding reception)!
  • <u>We are like the bridesmaids</u>. Are we ready for him? People who are
    ready will have a great time at the party. People who are not ready are
    going to miss the party... What can we do to be ready?

ACTIVITIES: **1. Clay Lamps**

(This activity could be hazardous if not properly supervised. If in doubt, just
get a leader to light one lamp.) Provide clay <u>or</u> salt-dough, but check it is not
flammable first! Give each youngster a lump of clay. Have them roll it into a
ball and make it into a small, fairly shallow cup shape – make sure that it will
not leak or spill! (If you do not want to keep the lamps afterwards, they do not
need to be thoroughly dry before use, as long as the dough is fairly stiff.)
Make wicks by twisting a small piece of cotton wool. Soak the wicks in
cooking oil. Fill the lamps with cooking oil and add the wick. Light them
carefully.

2. Ready for the Wedding

In advance, get together a set of props for each team, (eg pens, paper and an
envelope; slices of bread & sandwich filling; some remnants of material or
newspaper; a hymn book, artificial flowers etc). Ask your youngsters to get
into teams of about six. Tell each team that they have 15 minutes to get ready
for a wedding (eg send out an invitation, write the list of wedding presents,
prepare the food, get dressed up, choose the hymns, arrange the flowers...
and any other tasks anyone can think of!). Award a prize to the team which
has organised the best wedding in the time available.

KEY VERSE: *[Jesus said:] "So always be ready because you don't know the day or the hour*
the Son of Man will come". Matthew 25:13

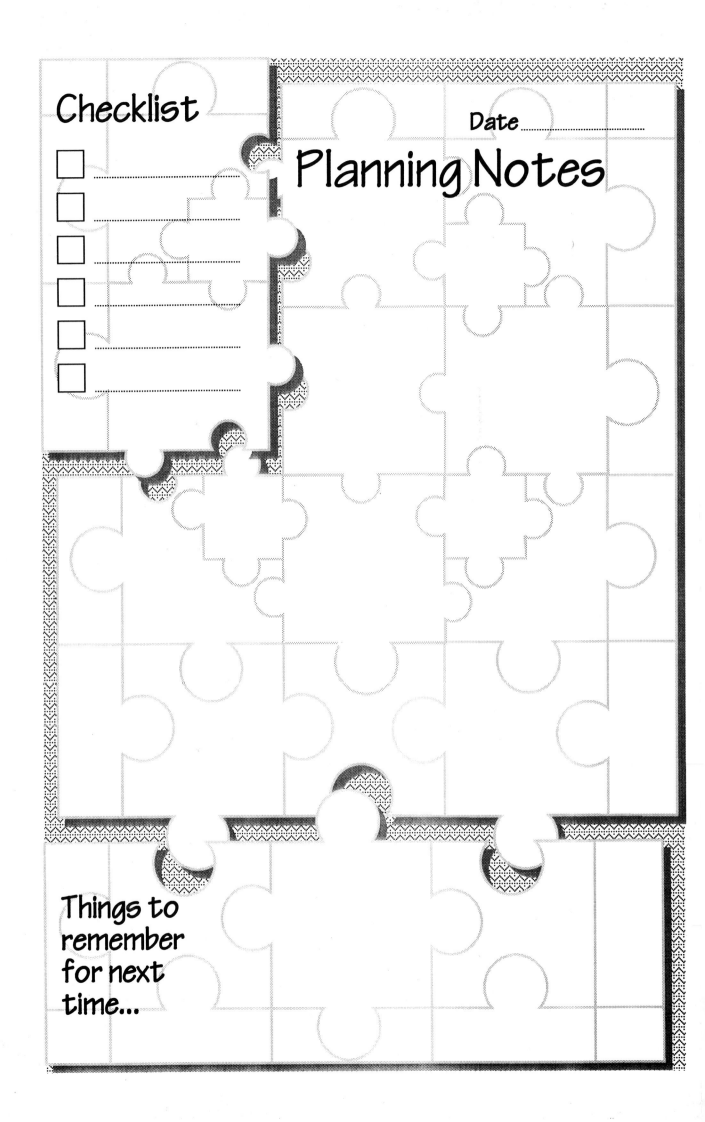

Checklist

Date

Planning Notes

Things to
remember
for next
time...